Alcohol in the USSR

Duke Press Policy Studies

The Political Reliability of the Warsaw Pact Armies
The Southern Tier
Ivan Volgyes

Afghanistan and the Soviet Union
Henry S. Bradsher

Population and Development in Rural Egypt
Allen C. Kelley, Atef M. Khalifa, *and* M. Nabil el-Khorazaty

Power and Protest in the Countryside
Studies of Rural Unrest in Asia, Europe, and Latin America
Edited by Robert P. Weller *and* Scott E. Guggenheim

Alcohol in the USSR

A Statistical Study

Vladimir G. Treml

Published in cooperation with the

Center of Alcohol Studies,
Rutgers University

Duke Press Policy Studies

Durham, N.C., 1982

Library of Congress Cataloging in Publication Data

Treml, Vladimir G.
  Alcohol in the USSR.

  (Duke Press policy studies)
  "Published in cooperation with the Center
of Alcohol Studies, Rutgers University."
  Bibliography: p.
  Includes index.
  1. Alcoholism—Soviet Union—Statistics.
2. Liquor traffic—Soviet Union—Statistics.
I. Rutgers Center of Alcohol Studies.
II. Title. III. Title: Alcohol in the U.S.S.R.
IV. Series.
  HV5513.T73   1982   362.2'922'0947   82-9625
  ISBN 0-8223-0484-8

Contents

Tables

Foreword

The work of Professor Treml on alcoholism in the USSR is pioneering in more than one way. When he began his work in the early 1970s neither Soviet nor Western literature offered any summary data on production, distribution, or consumption of alcohol in the USSR. In the remarkable research effort which culminated in this monograph, Treml defined the problems of measurement, developed the necessary estimation techniques, and gave us an invaluable set of reliable and cross-checked statistics on state produced and home distilled alcohol in the USSR, finally lifting the veil of secrecy which had covered the subject for several decades. Of particular interest is the fact that the data offered in this monograph are both in rubles and physical terms enabling the analyst to examine not only per capita consumption in liters but also state revenues, tax burdens, and family expenditure on alcohol in the country as a whole and by republic.

The importance of having the data on per capita consumption of alcohol cannot be overstressed as they help us to understand the remarkable turnaround in demographic trends in the past decade and a half in the USSR. From a pattern of continually declining death rates, we now find that the crude death rate in the USSR has increased by 50 percent between 1964 and 1980. From a pattern of remarkable decreases in infant mortality between 1950 and 1971, as officially reported, we now find that infant mortality rates apparently increased by 50 percent in the last decade. From a pattern of increasing life expectancy for males and females until the mid-1960s, we now find a dramatic drop in male life expectancy at age zero (of about four years) and in female life expectancy (about one year). In each of these issues, one of the main culprits is alcohol abuse. Thus, Treml's work provides the statistical underpinning to the various adverse demographic measures just noted. The constrained, and sometimes not so constrained, references in the Soviet literature to problems ensuing from excess alcohol consumption—premature male mortality, the high share of infant deaths and mentally retarded children born to chronically alcoholic women, the lack of age data from the 1979 census of population (now three years afterward)—attest to the dramatic consequences of this pattern of alcohol abuse endemic to the Soviet scene.

The present work, in combination with other efforts by Treml, provides a major contribution to our understanding of the impact of heavy drinking, especially of strong beverages, on health and on vital statistics (crude death rates, infant mortality) in the USSR. For example, the regional differences for alcohol consumption contained in this study allow us to adduce evidence for alternative materials on differential mortality rates for the RSFSR relative to Central Asia as follows: In the RSFSR, the average per capita consumption of all alcoholic beverages for persons fifteen years of age and over in 1967 was 6.32 liters per annum, whereas in the Central Asian region it was one-third that level, at 2.13 liters. Simultaneously, he also provides crucial data for analysis of the overall situation (in table 6.1) by demonstrating that strong beverages (hard liquor) comprises a remarkable share of the adjusted pure alcohol content of all consumption. Although the share of strong beverage consumption has decreased from about 85 percent in 1955 to about 60 percent in 1979, this latter share is 50 percent greater than the corresponding share in the United States—and hard liquor is just that, harder on the physiology and health of the individual. In a large number of countries, western as well as eastern, alcoholism remains a problem or is becoming an even greater problem. The Soviets, however, have a special problem because of the hard liquor factor within the overall structure of their alcohol consumption and Treml provides abundant evidence for this.

Thus, Treml's work will make a lasting contribution to our understanding of the Soviet economy and society.

Murray Feshbach

Georgetown University

Preface

The purpose of this study is to present a set of statistics on the production and consumption of alcoholic beverages in the USSR in the 1955–1979 period.

Soviet authorities and the media openly admit that excessive drinking and alcoholism pose a very serious social, economic, and health problem for Soviet society, but the statistical and other data necessary for an analysis and assessment of the magnitude of the problem and its changes over time are completely absent from the available literature and standard statistical sources. Such important measures as per capita consumption of alcohol and alcohol mortality have not been published for about fifty years. Time series on ethanol and vodka production and on retail sales of alcoholic beverages have either gradually disappeared from statistical sources or have been concealed in various ways since the early 1960s.

The absence of data is not complete, however. Some output series which were banned from national statistical sources continued to be reported in regional publications. Assorted statistics on production, alcohol content, shipments, taxes, prices, and retail trade in alcoholic beverages appear periodically in monographs and industrial journals. Using these fragmentary data and a variety of estimating techniques, it proved possible to construct very important sets of statistical data. This study, then, discusses and documents the step-by-step collation and interpretation of the available data and the methodology used in making various estimates.

The study covers production and consumption of different alcoholic beverages in rubles terms and in terms of alcohol content, prices, taxes, production of ethanol, the use of agricultural commodities in the ethanol industry, and illegal home production of various beverages. The last section is devoted to per capita consumption of alcohol and personal expenditures on alcoholic beverages. The coverage is by no means comprehensive since some important issues and phenomena related to alcoholism and alcohol abuse in the USSR turned out to be unreasearchable.

The impact of heavy drinking on labor productivity in the USSR must be significant, but the available data proved to be too ambiguous and inconsistent for any valid analysis. About all that can be said now is that the fragmentary data and anecdotal evidence given in the Soviet literature are consistent with the conclusion of two prominent Soviet economists who estimated that total abstinence would have resulted in a 10 percent increase in labor productivity [Strumilin and Sonin 1974]. Unfortunately this statement was not documented and the impact on labor productivity must remain unquantified.

Another aspect of alcoholism in the USSR which must remain open is the overall impact of drinking on the health of the Soviet population and on demographic trends in general. Western studies have conclusively demonstrated the link between high per capita consumption of alcohol and mortality, particularly male mortality, life expectancy, and infant mortality in the USSR [Dutton 1979 and 1981; Davis and Feshbach 1980].

However, without statistics on mortality and morbidity broken down into alcoholic psychoses, chronic and acute alcohol poisoning, alcoholic cirrhosis, and traffic and other accidents caused by drinking, the overall picture remains unclear. The author did succeed in estimating one element in the overall mortality statistics—deaths from acute alcohol poisoning. Working from time series on deaths from various poisons in the 1965–1976 period, which were published in the Soviet forensic medicine literature, it proved to be possible to estimate deaths from ingestion of alcohol and various fluids containing alcohol. According to these data, in 1976 some 39,800 people died in the USSR from acute alcohol poisoning. This rate of 15.9 deaths per 100,000 population is incredibly high by international standards; in the US in the same year the rate of death from alcohol poisoning was 0.18 and the world average was probably only slightly higher [Treml 1981 and 1983 forthcoming]. But fatal alcohol poisoning is only one of several components of alcohol mortality and much more research will be required before we can have a comprehensive picture.

Regrettably, without reasonably accurate statistics on the impact of alcoholism on labor productivity and on health and vital demographic rates, we cannot evaluate the overall economic and social cost of alcohol abuse in the USSR. However, indirect evidence and brief, obscure references in Soviet literature suggest that these costs are huge and continuously growing.

The seriousness of alcohol-related problems is not, of course, a novel theme in the Western literature. A number of excellent studies published in the last ten years have described the phenomena involved and analyzed the social, economic, psychological, and legal facets of the alcohol problem and their implications [Connor 1971, 1972, and 1979; Field and Powell 1981, Keller and Efron 1974: Powell 1983 forthcoming; Segal 1976]. However, analysis offered by the authors did not cover the quantitative dimensions of the problem and it is hoped that this study will complement their efforts.

A major statistical project of this nature requires a certain sequence both in preparation of the data and in the discussion and analysis of them. Thus, production statistics must be compiled before the sales statistics can be properly interpreted, and the data on the alcohol content of various beverages must be tabulated before the estimates of consumption of pure alcohol can be made. The organization of this study thus strictly follows the sequence in which the actual research was carried out and the estimates were made. The reader interested in the final results of this study may simply go through all the major tables. However, complete and comprehensive description and documentation are still necessary to enable the more demanding analyst to examine the evidence and to form his own conclusions concerning the reliability of the estimates.

Partial funding for this study was provided by the Duke University Research Council and the "Second Economy in the USSR" project conducted at the University of California (Berkeley) and Duke University under a Ford Foundation grant. I am particularly grateful to Professor Gregory Grossman, the principal investigator of the project, for his encouragement and assistance. Results of a survey of recent Soviet émigrés made under the auspices of this project proved to be invaluable for several parts of the study.

Thanks are due to my wife, Emma, to Michael Alexeev, Keith Bush, Murray Feshbach, Dimitry Gallik, Paul Goldberg, Leonid Khotin, Boris Segal, and to a number of my other colleagues and students, too numerous to be listed, whose help ranged from reading and commenting on the manuscript, to obtaining scarce Soviet sources, and to copying price labels in Moscow liquor stores—not an ideal place for research. The errors and omissions are, of course, my own responsibility.

An earlier version of this study was presented and discussed by Professor Christopher Davis at the conference on "Economic Aspects of the Use and Misuse of Alcohol" held at the University of Essex in November 1981.

Vladimir G. Treml

March 1982

Alcohol in the USSR

1. Production and Supply of Alcoholic Beverages in the Soviet Union

1.1 *General Notes*

This section covers production, foreign trade, and supply of alcoholic beverages measured in physical quantities. The standard Soviet three-group classification of alcoholic beverages will be employed:
1. Vodka and vodka-based beverages, including cordials, and liqueurs, as well as pure drinking alcohol;
2. Wine, including grape wines, fruit and berry wines, champagne, and cognac;
3. Beer.

The same three-group classification applies to industry designations: thus, vodka and vodka-based beverages are produced by the vodka and alcohol industry; and beer is produced by the "beer and nonalcoholic beverages" industry. All three industries as well as the industry producing ethanol are parts of the food industry directed by the Food Ministry of the USSR. Small quantities of wine and beer are produced in enterprises of the cooperative trade organizations, and these will be counted within the various totals given here.

The Soviet Union also produces small quantities of gin, rum, and whiskey, but in the absence of any additional information we will assume that these beverages are classified within the vodka group. The traditional Russian kvas (bread-based beverages) and other mild beverages containing less than 2 percent alcohol by volume are classified with nonalcoholic beverages. Technically speaking, the entire alcohol output should be classified as a product of state industries. Clearly, illegally distilled home-brewed spirits such as samogon would not enter state retail trade outlets, and its production and sales will be estimated elsewhere in this study. However, certain quantities of both grape and fruit wines produced by collective farms and / or peasants could conceivably enter either production or consumption statistics. This is a gray area of the analysis where estimates would be too time-consuming and, probably, not too reliable. Accordingly, the whole issue is dismissed on the assumption that the quantities involved are small. Thus, for all practical purposes statistics on production and consumption are to be taken as state-produced and state-taxed alcoholic beverages.

On several occasions Soviet authorities expressed their intention to reduce the output of alcoholic beverages, particularly of strong beverages such as vodka, but the output statistics summarized in table 1.1 clearly do not bear this out. In fact, only a temporary reduction in the output of vodka in 1959 and 1960 can be directly traced to the government antidrinking campaign, and specifically to the 20 percent increase in prices of vodka. The reduction in the output of vodka in 1971 is explained by bad agricultural harvests; the output resumed its growth with the good grain harvest of 1973. Similarly, reductions in output of grape wines in the 1955–1979 period always coincided with poor grape harvests.

The decline in the output of beer after 1978[1] is somewhat puzzling. One of the main efforts of the antialcoholism policy of the Soviet government was to encourage consumption of beer and wines at the expense of vodka. Annual consumption of beer in the USSR of about 30 liters per person fifteen years old and older is much lower than in most countries, and according to many reports demand for beer is not satisified in a number of areas. Nevertheless the insufficient domestic production of barley and hops and the need to import them was apparently a sufficient reason to cut beer production in 1979.

In brief, the output of alcoholic beverages summarized in table 1.1 shows that steady growth and minor fluctuations observed in some years are explained by considerations of economic expediency and not by government-directed restraint.

1.2 Vodka

In accordance with the standard Soviet commodity classification, this group includes vodka (a mixture of ethanol with water and a few additives, such as sugar) and a large variety of vodka-based beverages such as cordials, liqueurs, and flavored vodkas. Output statistics for 1955–1962 are from *Promyshlennost'* [1964, pp. 454–455], for 1963–1965 from Klemenchuk and Popov [1967, p. 68], and for 1966–1967 from Krasikov [1977, p. 118]. The USSR annual statistical handbooks *Narodnoe khoziaistvo* ceased publication of vodka output in 1963, but various republican handbooks continued to do so until the late 1970s. The share of nine republics (the RSFSR, the Ukraine, Belorussia, Moldavia, Lithuania, Latvia, Estonia, Azerbaidzhan, and Armenia) was an almost constant 91.2 percent of the total USSR output in the years for which both republican and national totals were available. In 1975 the reported annual productive capacity of these republics was almost the same 91.29 percent of the USSR total [Kochubeeva 1977, p. 59]. The estimates for 1968 and later years are thus based on an assumption of constancy of republican shares and the available regional output data. In the late 1970s most republican statistical sources stopped publishing the data on vodka output. Through 1976 the estimates can be considered reliable, but the margin of probable error increased in 1977 and 1978 and particularly in 1979 when the output data disappeared from the RSFSR annual statistical handbooks.

1.3 Grape Wine

Statistics on grape wine are as published in standard Soviet statistical sources.

1.4 Fruit and Berry Wines

The 1958 and 1965 output data are from Zaiats, et al. [1969, p. 25] with the missing years estimated by linear interpolation. The 1966–1969 output data are as re-

Table 1.1. Domestic production of alcoholic beverages by type, 1955-1979, millions of liters

	Vodka	Grape wine	Fruit & berry wines	Champagne	Cognac	Beer
1955	1,169	474	130	19.7	17.00	1,847
1956	1,225	509	151	21.9	16.00	1,807
1957	1,402	552	154	23.8	12.00	1,965
1958	1,454	618	169	26.0	12.25	1,991
1959	1,373	669	185	28.0	13.64	2,319
1960	1,381	777	203	29.9	15.02	2,498
1961	1,457	848	222	32.1	17.80	2,667
1962	1,620	1,008	243	35.3	20.57	2,818
1963	1,689	1,186	265	37.4	23.38	2,807
1964	1,765	1,271	291	40.7	25.23	2,830
1965	1,888	1,339	318	44.7	27.15	3,169
1966	1,987	1,586	328	48.6	29.01	3,437
1967	2,136	1,800	350	53.7	30.13	3,613
1968	2,266	1,913	410	58.3	36.55	3,830
1969	2,383	2,402	453	63.4	44.33	3,970
1970	2,412	2,680	510	69.4	53.61	4,190
1971	2,343	2,800	580	74.7	56.80	4,410
1972	2,215	2,930	700	80.5	60.20	4,690
1973	2,474	2,070	1,100	86.7	63.90	5,080
1974	2,525	2,670	1,500	93.1	67.70	5,400
1975	2,630	2,970	1,600	104.3	72.00	5,710
1976	2,670	3,150	2,000	112.7	72.72	5,920
1977	2,740	3,070	2,100	121.0	73.44	6,190
1978	2,850	2,470	2,205	130.0	74.17	6,410
1979	2,850	2,940	2,315	139.0	74.91	6,333

ported in *Bolshaia Sovetskaia Entsiklopedia* [3rd ed., vol. 5, p. 861; hereinafter cited as BSE]. Starting with 1970 the output statistics become less reliable, apparently as an increasing share of fruit and berry wines was being produced outside the wine-making enterprises of the food industry. According to one source [Varibus, et al., 1976, p. 267], total output of fruit and berry wine was reaching 200 million liters. We will accept this figure for 1976 and estimate the output in the 1970–1975 period on the basis of production in five republics (RSFSR, LiSSR, LaSSR, ESSR, and BSSR), which has been regularly reported in republican handbooks, the output of fruit and berry wines in the food industry alone [Storchevoi 1975, p. 3; Zaiats, et al., 1979, pp. 24–25], and various other sources such as Struev, 1974, p. 12.

1.5 Champagne

Soviet statistics on production of champagne are usually given in bottles which have been converted to liters on the basis of 0.8 liters per bottle. Output data for 1955–1963 are from *Promyshlennost'* [1957, p. 407, and 1964, p. 457], for 1964–

1965 from Tartakovskii [1966, p. 10], and for 1966–1969 from BSE [3rd ed., Vol. 5, p. 86]. The 1970 output was recorded in "Vinogradstvo" [1972, pp. 2–8], 1974 output in Avdonin and Burshtein [1975, pp. 55–66], 1975 and 1977 output in Zaiats, et al.,[1979, pp. 24–25]. The output of champagne for the few missing years was estimated by interpolation.

1.6 *Cognac*

Output data for 1955–1957 are from Zotov [1958, p. 162], for 1958–1963 from Tartakovskii [1966, p. 10], 1966–1967 from Zaiats, et al. [1969, p. 26], and for 1970, 1975, and 1977 from Zaiats,et al. [1979, pp. 23–24, and p. 365]. Output for years for which no data were found was estimated by linear interpolation.

1.7 *Beer*

Statistics on beer are as published in standard Soviet statistical sources.

1.8 *Export and Import of Alcoholic Beverages*

Soviet annual statistical sources on foreign trade, *Vneshniaia torgovlia SSSR*, started to publish the breakdown of exported alcoholic beverages by type only in 1970. The quantities exported were small—thus in 1972 export of vodka composed 0.3 percent, export of wine 0.9 percent, and export of cognac 1.9 percent of domestic production. Judging from the value of total exports, their share in total domestic production was even smaller in earlier years. Thus the estimates, no matter how approximate, will not affect the main results of this study.

Under the circumstances, the estimates in liters for the 1955–1969 period were made as follows. Based on the trend in the post-1970 data, the export of cognac was estimated to increase by two-percentage-points per year. Based similarly on post-1970 data, exports of vodka and wine were assumed to constitute a constant 36 and 23 percent of the value of exports respectively. The value data thus estimated were converted to liters on the basis of average 1970–1972 prices. In some years export of wine was reported in tons and these were converted to liters on the basis of 1,000 liters per ton. For years in which export of high quality wines was reported in bottles, these were converted to liters at the rate of 0.75 liters per bottle [*Eksportno-Importnyi slovar'*, 1952, vol. 1, p. 359]. Export statistics are shown in table 1.2. Soviet imports of alcoholic beverages derived from standard statistical sources are shown in table 1.3.

As can be seen from the data in tables 1.1, 1.2, and 1.3 the Soviet Union is a net exporter of vodka and a net importer of rum, cognac, beer, and wine but only the last is of practical importance. In the late 1970s net imports of wine (import less export) composed about a quarter of domestic production. Foreign trade in finished products does not give us a complete picture of the importance of foreign markets for the Soviet alcoholic beverage industry, so we must consider foreign sources, which play an increasingly important role in supplying intermediate inputs into the production of cognac and beer in the USSR.

Table 1.2. Export of alcoholic beverages by type, thousands of liters

	Vodka	Wine	Cognac
1955	4,366	11,400	
1956	842	2,200	
1957	897	2,343	
1958	2,068	5,400	
1959	2,566	6,700	
1960	3,064	8,000	
1961	3,943	10,296	
1962	4,912	12,826	
1963	5,878	15,348	
1964	4,284	11,187	
1965	2,911	7,600	
1966	5,411	14,126	
1967	6,663	17,400	255
1968	7,329	19,135	513
1969	7,689	20,080	784
1970	7,754	27,454	1,006
1971	9,444	25,485	1,610
1972	12,334	33,608	2,293
1973	14,117	9,643	3,301
1974	15,804	11,071	3,598
1975	15,328	13,585	2,937
1976	17,172	13,795	3,156
1977	18,110	12,494	3,147
1978	20,129	14,521	3,581
1979	23,106	12,193	3,607

Throughout the period of this study, the USSR has been importing large quantities of cognac spirits, i.e., ethanol distilled from grape wine, from Rumania, Hungary, Bulgaria, Spain, and other countries. Using an average rate of output of 1.7 liters cognac of 42 percent alcohol per 1 kg of cognac spirits with average alcohol content of 65 percent [*Eksportno-Importnyi slovar'*, vol. 1, 1952, pp. 643–644], and assuming that all imported cognac spirits were used in domestic production, we can estimate that practically all Soviet output of cognac from the late 1950s to the late 1960s was produced with imported spirits. After the grape-growing republic of Moldavia began producing cognac in the 1960s, the ratio declined, but in the 1970s still better than half the total domestic output of Soviet cognac was made with imported cognac spirits.

Import of beer is not significant—less than 1 percent of domestic production. However, the Soviet beer industry relies heavily on imported malt, hops, and to a lesser extent, barley.

The USSR is producing millions of tons of different varieties of barley, but only a very small fraction can be used in beer brewing, and barley procured for the beer industry is often substandard in terms of the required quality [Balashov 1979, p. 16 and p. 76; Balashov 1976, pp. 106–107]. As a result better quality barley has been

Table 1.3. Import of alcoholic beverages by type, thousands of liters

	Vodka	Liqueurs	Rum	Wine	Cognac	Beer
1955				22,900		
1956				38,700		1,000
1957				37,600		2,000
1958			650	37,100		15,000
1959			1,200	33,900		23,000
1960			4,900	56,700		23,000
1961			5,763	57,100		26,000
1962			3,401	55,000		25,000
1963	699	1,133	3,446	74,500		15,000
1964	4,227	2,564	4,347	106,100		17,000
1965	5,054	2,055	5,607	128,200		18,000
1966	3,358	2,746	3,270	129,200		29,000
1967	5,481	2,039	4,184	179,800		28,000
1968	6,623	1,824	8,135	271,600		24,000
1969	8,639	1,568	6,801	683,700		20,000
1970	10,326	1,348	3,876	719,300		22,000
1971	5,936	2,248	8,989	771,800		25,000
1972	3,345	2,410	19,966	794,825		34,000
1973	1,761	2,299	14,060	686,425	8,948	30,000
1974	3,059	2,129	10,591	778,425	10,423	34,000
1975	3,390	4,419	11,900	869,648	15,550	41,280
1976	5,334	4,650	12,370	794,245	8,650	58,180
1977	9,201	4,619	13,470	659,590	6,300	74,140
1978	10,153	3,586	12,290	603,344	5,590	74,470
1979	7,156	5,668	12,630	708,157	6,450	68,870

periodically imported, although the quantities have been relatively small—less than one percent of the total requirement of the beer industry. Shortages of barley are covered by imported barley malt. In the early 1960s imported barley malt composed about 5 percent of total malt used, and the share increased to about 9 percent in the late 1960s. In the 1970s the dependence of Soviet beer breweries on imported malt continued to increase, averaging some 14 percent of domestic needs and reaching as much as 20 percent in some years.[2]

The overall dependence of the Soviet beer industry on imported hops is more difficult to evaluate because of serious gaps in the available data on domestic output and on imports. In the early 1960s the share of imported hops in the total quantity used fluctuated between 16 and 30 percent.[3] Between 1966 and 1973 the available Soviet foreign trade statistics do not show figures for the import of hops. This does not mean that they were not imported: the published Soviet foreign trade statistics have always been selective and certain foreign trade transactions have been periodically concealed. Since 1974 imported hops have reappeared in the published statistics, not in the list of total goods imported but buried in the individual-country data, mainly as imports from the US and Czechoslovakia. The sum of imports from these two countries (which in all probability does not cover all imports) fluctuated between 10 and 27 percent of total domestic needs.

Table 1.4. Supply of alcoholic beverages available for domestic consumption by type, millions of liters

	Vodka	Grape wine	Fruit & berry wines	Champagne	Cognac	Beer
1955	1,165	461	130	19.7	17.00	1,847
1956	1,224	518	151	21.9	16.00	1,808
1957	1,401	558	154	23.8	12.00	1,967
1958	1,452	617	169	26.0	12.25	2,006
1959	1,371	661	185	28.0	13.64	2,342
1960	1,383	784	203	29.9	15.02	2,521
1961	1,459	850	222	32.1	17.80	2,693
1962	1,618	998	243	35.3	20.57	2,843
1963	1,688	1,183	265	37.4	23.38	2,822
1964	1,767	1,298	291	40.7	25.23	2,845
1965	1,893	1,386	318	44.7	27.15	3,187
1966	1,987	1,616	328	48.6	29.01	3,466
1967	2,136	1,864	350	53.7	29.88	3,641
1968	2,268	2,057	410	58.3	36.04	3,854
1969	2,384	2,570	453	63.4	43.55	3,990
1970	2,409	3,203	510	69.4	52.60	4,212
1971	2,345	3,369	580	74.7	55.19	4,435
1972	2,225	3,507	700	80.5	57.91	4,724
1973	2,476	2,608	1,100	36.7	69.55	5,110
1974	2,522	3,265	1,500	93.1	74.52	5,434
1975	2,634	3,635	1,600	104.3	84.61	5,751
1976	2,675	3,734	2,000	112.7	78.21	5,978
1977	2,749	3,531	2,100	121.0	76.59	6,261
1978	2,856	2,906	2,205	130.0	76.17	6,484
1979	2,852	3,635	2,315	139.0	77.75	6,402

Soviet beer production is clearly experiencing difficulties. In the 1955–1974 period the output was steadily growing at about 10 percent per year. And the 1975–1980 plan called for an ambitious target of 8,450 million liters, implying another increase of almost 50 percent [Balashov 1979, p. 5]. However, the actual output in 1980 was reported as 6,130 million liters or some 27 percent below the planned figure. The inability to provide the necessary inputs from domestic sources is the probable explanation.

1.9 *Supply of Alcoholic Beverages for Domestic Consumption*

The supply of alcoholic beverages for domestic consumption is estimated in this study as domestic output less export plus import (tables 1.1, 1.2, and 1.3). Following the standard Soviet classification the imported liqueurs and rum are added to the vodka group. One adjustment appears necessary at this point. Wine manufacturing is a complex process involving production, mixing of different types, fortification with alcohol, filtering, storing, and bottling, and most of which involve some losses [Tartakovskii 1966, pp. 54–69]. A certain share of new wine is also put aside for aging, although in the case of the Soviet wine industry it is probably a rather small share. Finally, some wine may turn out to be defective while in warehouses or retail trade outlets and will be destroyed. It is, of course, possible that losses are netted out at the manufacturer's level, and some undoubtedly are. However, knowing the Soviet preference for gross measures, one can expect that not all losses are written off, and furthermore some occur after the wine is shipped. Using some information given in the source cited above, we will reduce the total supply of wine by 5 percent to account for these losses in all years.

Some losses of this type occur probably at various stages between the producing industry and the final buyer in other beverages. However, stronger beverages such as vodka or cognac are not as likely to spoil and the controls are also tighter. In the absence of any additional information no adjustment will be made.

The supply of alcoholic beverages available for domestic consumption as defined in this study is shown in table 1.4.

2. Alcohol Content and The Consumption of Alcoholic Beverages

2.1. General Notes

In order to analyze total and per capita consumption of alcohol in the USSR, we have to estimate the average alcohol content of different beverages. Average alcohol content by type is also important in the investigation of general trends in consumption. Thus, as will be shown below, the share of strong alcoholic beverages (40 percent alcohol content and higher) converted to absolute alcohol has been gradually declining in the USSR. On the other hand, the average alcohol content of wines has been steadily increasing.

The data on alcohol content of specific beverages are relatively easy to find; the most serious difficulty lies with the mix of different beverages within the given group. The alcohol content of various beverages was estimated on the basis of a variety of sources, and these estimates rest, in some cases, on fairly restrictive assumptions. It must be stressed that the entire set of estimates was checked as much as possible against other data such as the production of food-based ethanol, sales of beverages in retail trade, and the mix of different beverages. The estimates made in this section are not summarized in a single table but are given in each subsection.

2.2. Alcohol Content of Vodka and Vodka-Based Beverages

The various estimates of alcohol content of different vodkas and vodka-based beverages are derived from a variety of sources and rest on certain assumptions. Some comparison with control variables was also possible as will be discussed below.

The separation of vodkas proper from vodka-based beverages is made on the basis of the reported share of vodka of 94 percent in 1950 [Kerashev 1971, p. 79,], 87.6 percent in 1963 [Pykhov 1964, p. 6], 84.2 percent in 1965 ["Spirtovaia" 1965, p. 2], and 82.4 percent in 1967 [Kerashev 1971, p. 79]. Shares of vodka in the whole group for years for which no information is available were estimated by interpolation. It will be noticed that the decrease of the share of vodkas proper proceeded much faster in the 1963–1967 period than in the 1950–1963 period. It is probably explained by rapid phasing out of inexpensive "Vodka" vodka [Pychov 1964, p. 6]. By 1967 the production of "Vodka" practically ceased, and we will assume that the share of 82.4 percent remained constant for the next ten years.

The alcohol industry is producing a great variety of vodkas, ranging in alcohol content from the standard 40 percent to the strong 56 percent; pure 95 percent drinking ethanol is also produced and marketed in some areas, particularly in the

Table 2.1. Alcoholic content of vodka-based liqueurs and cordials

Type	Alcohol content
Bitter "nastoiki" (strong)	35-45%
Bitter "nastoiki" (standard)	25-30
Semi-sweet "nastoiki"	25-30
Average	31.7
"Nalivki" (sweet)	17-20
Average	18.5
Strong liqueurs	33-45
Dessert liqueurs	25-30
Cream liqueurs	20-23
Average	29.3

North and Far East. However, the bulk of output consists of the standard 40 percent vodkas [BSE 3rd ed., vol. 5, p. 175; Kovalenko et al., 1974, pp. 87–88; Varibus et al., 1976, pp. 241–242]. Judging from the increasingly rapid introduction of vodkas stronger than 40 percent, we must assume that the average alcohol content of the vodka group as a whole continued to rise.

The large variety of vodka-based liquers and cordials produced in the USSR are broken down into three types: "Nastoiki," "nalivki," and liqueurs. The information on the alcohol content of these beverages was collected from several sources [Varibus et al., 1976, p. 244; Sivolap et al., 1954, pp. 118–119; Zadorozhnyi, ed., 1975, pp. 81–82; Kudentsov 1975, pp. 330–331; Kovalenko 1974, pp. 89–92; Mel'man et al., 1966, pp. 133–137; Khomutov 1970, pp. 126–128; Mitiukov 1974, pp. 52–53]. Most sources provide identical information, although there is some evidence that the alcohol content given in sources published in recent years is somewhat higher. The overall picture derived from these sources is shown in table 2.1.

Three different sources [Pykhov 1964, p. 6; "Spirtovaia" 1965; and Nazarian 1972, p. 26] give distribution of vodka-based liqueurs for 1963, 1965, and 1967 which show that on the average "nastoiki" accounted for 81 percent of the total for the group, "nalivki" composed 16 percent and liqueurs proper about 3 percent. Using the averages derived above and these percentages as weights, we estimate the average alcohol content of the entire group at 30 percent. It may be noted that the average alcohol content of 30 percent for the vodka-based beverages in the 1960s was only slightly higher than the pre-war average alcohol content of about 28 percent (estimated on the basis of Zotov [1958, pp. 110–114], Zotov et al., [1967, p. 398], and Kochubeeva and Shtainer [1974, p. 10]).

We will assume that the average alcohol content of the vodka group was 40.5 in 1955 and was growing by 0.1 percent per year, reaching 42.2 percent by 1972. In 1972 the authorities prohibited production and sales of vodkas of 50 and 56 percent alcohol content and ostensibly tried to discourage sales of other strong vodka-based beverages. The results of the 1972 ordinance were mixed—while the production of some strong vodkas was discontinued, foreign observers and the Soviet

Table 2.2. Average alcoholic content of all vodka-based beverages

Year	Alcohol content, percent	Year	Alcohol content, percent	Year	Alcohol content, percent
1955	39.6	1964	39.9	1973	38.9
1956	39.6	1965	39.7	1974	38.7
1957	39.7	1966	39.7	1975	38.7
1958	39.7	1967	39.6	1976	38.7
1959	39.8	1968	39.7	1977	38.7
1960	39.8	1969	39.8	1978	38.7
1961	39.8	1970	39.9	1979	38.7
1962	39.9	1971	40.0		
1963	39.9	1972	40.1		

literature continued to reveal expanding sales of 43 and 45 percent vodkas. Sales of 95 percent ethanol for drinking purposes also continued. Almost arbitrarily, we will estimate the alcohol content of vodkas after 1972 at 41 percent to reflect these changes.

We will assume that the average alcohol content of vodka-based beverages remained at the same level of 30 percent from 1955 through the early 1970s. In 1972 the Soviet authorities began to encourage consumption of substitutes for vodka such as wine and the so-called "low-alcohol" beverages, defined as having alcohol content of 30 percent and less. Thus, the share of these "low-alcohol" beverages in the output of vodka and vodka-based beverages in the RSFSR rose from about 2 percent in 1972 to 7 percent in 1973, and to 8 percent in 1974 [Arens 1975, p. 2]. However, the increase in production and consumption of low-alcohol beverages was not sustained for very long, because after the mid-1970s newspapers complained about the insufficient supply of these beverages. A recent article noted the low output levels of several more popular beverages of alcohol content of 25 percent and lower [Kramarskii and Boiko 1979, p. 2]. Based on this evidence we will estimate that the average alcohol content of vodka-based beverages dropped to 29 percent in 1973 and remained at the level of 28 percent starting in 1974.

The combined-average alcohol content of the vodka and vodka-based beverage group is then estimated in table 2.2.

2.3. Alcohol Content of Grape Wines

The Soviet wine industry is producing more than 600 types of grape wines [Zaiats et al., 1969, p. 25], and, therefore, the estimation of the mix of different types and their alcohol content will be subject to error. The somewhat simplified classification of wines in table 2.1 will be used in this study (based on Tartakovskii [1966, pp. 21–22], Kovalenko, et al., [1974, pp. 26–51], BSE [3rd ed., vol. 5, p. 78], and Kruglikov [1971, pp. 39–42].

Table 2.3. Classification of Soviet wines by alcohol content

Type	Alcohol (range)	Content (%) (average)	Alcohol produced by natural fermentation (%)
Table wines			
Dry	9-14	11.5	all
Semi-Dry	9-12	10.5	all
Fortified wines			
Dessert (sweet)	12-17	14.5	not less than 1.2
Strong	17-20	18.5	not less than 3.0
Aromatic and misc.	12-18	15.0	not known

We have a fairly detailed breakdown of wines by type for the 1960–1968 period [*Vestnik statistiki*, No. 6, 1969, p. 89] and information for selected years, with all the data tabulated below. There are two possible sources of error in the calculations of the average alcohol content of Soviet wines. First, most if not all information on the distribution of wine by type refers to wines produced by the wine industry of the Ministry of Food, which gives no data on other wines produced in collective farms or in other industries. We must assume that the distribution is the same for all wines. The second possible source of error lies in the nature of the available data: even though the estimated content of Soviet wines is based on production statistics, this estimate will be applied to consumption statistics, which are somewhat different because of export and import of wines, losses of wine between wine producing enterprises and the market, and the storing of wine for aging. The estimation of the average alcohol content of Soviet grape wines must be done in two stages: first the distribution of wine by type must be ascertained; then the average alcohol content by type must be determined.

The available data on the distribution of wine by type are presented in table 2.4. They are derived from Zotov [1958, p. 121 and p. 190], *Vestnik statistiki* [No. 6, 1969, p. 89], Zotov [1967, p. 378], and Zaiats et al., [1979, p. 25]. The years for which no data were reported (1957–1959, 1969, 1971–1973, and 1975 and later) were estimated by interpolation. We will assume that the average alcohol content of dry and semi-dry table wines remains unchanged for this entire period at 11.5 and 10.5 percent, respectively. This assumption is not warranted in the case of fortified and aromatic wines, where available evidence suggests that the quantities of ethanol added to wines were increasing faster than the wine output. Thus, according to Pykhov [1969, pp. 28–29] the delivery of ethanol to the wine industry increased threefold in the 1960–1968 period while the output of grape wine increased 2.46 times and the output of fruit and berry wines doubled. We have less statistical data for 1970, but frequent reports in newspapers suggest that the trend has been away from low alcohol content table wines in favor of fortified wines with ever stronger alcohol content. [Struev 1974, p. 12; Dorofeev 1976, p. 13; Voina 1978, p. 12; Dorofeev 1979, p. 10; Shatunovskii 1980, p. 6; Man'ko 1980, p. 4].

We will use the following percentages for the alcohol content of fortified wines:

Table 2.4. Average alcohol content of grape wines

Year	Percent	Year	Percent	Year	Percent
1955	15.2	1964	16.2	1973	17.3
1956	15.2	1965	16.5	1974	17.4
1957	15.3	1966	16.7	1975	17.4
1958	15.4	1967	16.9	1976	17.5
1959	15.5	1968	17.1	1977	17.5
1960	15.6	1969	17.1	1978	17.6
1961	15.7	1970	17.2	1979	17.6
1962	15.9	1971	17.2		
1963	16.1	1972	17.3		

from 1955 to 1960 dessert wines contained 14 percent alcohol, strong wines 18 percent, and aromatic wines 14 percent; in the period since 1969, these figures have increased by 0.1 percent per year.

The share of naturally fermented alcohol is assumed to remain constant at 1.2 percent for dessert wines and 3 percent for strong and aromatic wines.

The estimates of average alcohol content for the entire grape wine group based on methods described above are shown in table 2.4.

2.4. Alcohol Content of Berry and Fruit Wines

Various fruit and berry wines produced in the USSR range in alcohol content from 10 to 18 percent, of which about 5.5 percent is produced by natural fermentation and the rest is added [BSE 3rd ed., vol. 5, p. 78, and Kovalenko, et al., 1974, pp. 51–55]. Various sources consulted in this study [Kudentsov 1975, p. 336; Varibus et al., 1976, pp. 267–269] yield an average of 15.5 percent alcohol content. The evidence in newspapers and reports of observers suggests that, as in the case of grape wines, the average alcohol content of fruit and berry wines was gradually increasing, particularly since the mid 1960s when the output statistics show the growing popularity of these fortified beverages. It is believed that 15.5 percent measures the average alcohol content of berry and fruit wines fairly accurately for the entire period. However, it is virtually impossible to estimate the rate of change over this period. We will use 15 percent for the 1955–1964 period, 15.5 for 1965, and increase by 0.1 percentage points every two years after that.

2.5. Alcohol Content of Miscellaneous Beverages

Champagne. The alcohol content of Soviet champagne ranges from 10.5 to 13.5 percent [Sivolap et al., 1954, p. 110; Varibus et al., 1976, pp. 266–267] so we will use the midpoint of this range, or 12 percent, for the entire period.

Cognac. The alcohol content of cognacs or brandy produced in the USSR ranges from 40 to 57 percent [Sivolap et al., 1954, p. 108; Tartakovskii 1966, p. 23;

Table 2.5. Total consumption of pure alcohol, millions of liters

	Strong beverages (supply)	All beverages (supply)	Adjustments for changes in stocks	Strong beverages (adjusted)	All beverages (adjusted)
1955	468.5	615.8	1.008	472.3	620.7
1956	491.4	649.7	.985	498.9	640.1
1957	461.2	731.6	1.006	564.6	736.0
1958	582.6	765.3	.919	535.4	703.3
1959	551.4	755.2	.993	547.5	749.9
1960	556.7	788.7	1.039	578.4	819.2
1961	588.2	839.6	1.022	601.1	857.7
1962	654.2	938.9	.993	649.6	932.3
1963	683.3	1,002.7	.985	673.1	987.7
1964	715.6	1,059.8	.977	699.2	1,035.4
1965	762.9	1,141.9	.981	748.4	1,120.2
1966	801.0	1,231.5	.986	789.8	1,245.0
1967	858.4	1,343.7	1.005	862.7	1,350.4
1968	917.8	1,456.1	1.011	927.9	1,472.1
1969	967.1	1,607.6	.992	959.4	1,594.7
1970	983.3	1,752.2	.942	926.3	1,650.6
1971	961.2	1,781.1	.969	931.4	1,725.9
1972	916.5	1,792.2	1.013	928.4	1,815.5
1973	963.2	1,761.0	1.019	981.5	1,794.5
1974	1,007.3	1,997.9	.976	983.1	1,850.0
1975	1,054.9	2,143.0	.996	1,050.7	2,134.4
1976	1,052.2	2,233.5	1.011	1,063.8	2,258.1
1977	1,096.0	2,268.5	.986	1,080.7	2,236.7
1978	1,137.3	2,225.5	1.009	1,127.2	2,245.5
1979	1,136.4	2,378.1	n.a.	1,136.4	2,378.1

n.a.: Data are not available.

Varibus et al., 1976, pp. 280–281], but mass-produced ordinary cognacs have an alcohol content of 40–41 percent [Shakhtan, ed., 1969, p. 268]. We will use 42% as the first approximation.

Beer. The alcohol content of Soviet beer ranges from 1.5 to 7 percent [Sivolap et al., 1954, p. 121; Zotov et al., 1967, p. 415; Varibus et al., 1976, p. 287]. The popular Zhiguli beer containing 2.8 percent alcohol composed some 90 percent of all beer produced in 1956 [Zotov 1958, p. 125] and its dominance has probably remained. We will use an average of 3.0 percent for the entire period.

2.6. Consumption of Alcohol

Having estimated the average alcohol content of all major types of beverages (sections 2.1–2.5 above) and the domestic supply of these beverages (table 2.3) we can proceed to calculate the total quantity of pure alcohol available for consumption. The calculations are shown in table 2.5, with the first column recording total alcohol supplied in the form of strong beverages (vodka-group and cognac) and the second column recording the total alcohol supplied in all beverages.

The supply figures may or may not correctly reflect consumption of alcohol in the country, because part of the supply may be added to the stocks and not consumed. Or consumption may be higher than supply with the additional quantities coming from existing stocks. Thus the supply data have to be adjusted to reflect changes in stocks of alcoholic beverages.

Unfortunately, the only data available on a regular basis are changes in stocks and inventories in retail trade measured in rubles. Therefore, we have to ignore the possible changes at the wholesale level in trade organizations and at producing enterprises. The possible error resulting from our inability to estimate inventory changes at these levels is probably not too great. The second assumption which must be made is that the mix of beverages by type held in retail inventories is identical to the mix of beverages in the supply of alcoholic beverages. That is, we will adjust the total quantity of alcohol supplied to consumers in any given year in proportion both to the ratio of change in inventories and to the sales of alcoholic beverages in rubles.

The formula used in the adjustment is:

$$Q(1 - \frac{D}{S + D}) = C$$

where

Q stands for the supply of alcohol in liters
D stands for the change (positive or negative) in inventories of alcoholic beverages in retail trade organizations measured in rubles
S stands for the sales of alcoholic beverages in retail trade measured in rubles
C stands for the consumption of alcohol in liters.

The data on sales and inventory changes are given in chapter 3, and the adjustment factors are shown in column 3, table 2.5. The last two columns show the consumption of pure alcohol in the form of strong alcoholic beverages and in the form of all beverages.

3. State Trade in Alcoholic Beverages: Prices, Sales, and Taxes

3.1. *General Notes*

Both production and sales of alcoholic beverages constitute a state monopoly in the USSR. This section deals with officially recorded sales in two types of trade organizations—consumer retail stores of the Ministry of Trade and the stores of the cooperative trade organizations. The differences between the two groups are essentially administrative and should not be of concern in this study.

A certain amount of consumer goods bypass the trade organizations (e.g., public utilities and certain other services), but all the Soviet literature on trade and distribution indicates that most consumer goods, including alcoholic beverages, enter consumption via retail trade, and thus sales can be equated with consumption. A certain quantity of processed foods and agricultural commodities is in fact sold in private farmers' markets, but all the evidence indicates that even low-alcohol-content beverages such as wines and beer are not traded in these markets. The whole phenomenon of illegally produced home-distilled samogon will be treated in a separate section of this paper.

One gray area of Soviet retail trade statistics is the so-called "special" or "hard-currency" stores. Foreign visitors to the USSR as well as some groups of Soviet citizens have access to "special" stores. In the case of foreign visitors, stores such as "Berezkas" sell goods, including alcoholic beverages, priced in rubles. In fact, the buyers are paying for the goods in foreign currencies exchanged for rubles at the official exchange rate in the store. The posted ruble prices are, as a rule, much lower than in open state stores.[1] The second group of stores serve Soviet citizens who have legal access to foreign currencies (Soviet citizens receiving funds from abroad, diplomats, and military personnel). In these stores the foreign currencies are converted to special coupons which can then be used for purchasing goods.

A search of the Soviet literature offers no clues to the statistical treatment of sales in these stores. Since prices posted in these stores are ruble prices, the sales conceivably could be included with retail trade statistics. On the other hand, ultimately these sales represent sales for foreign currencies and could be recorded as exports. Neither the quantities involved nor the statistical treatment of these sales are known and the whole issue must remain open.

3.2. *Retail Sales of Alcoholic Beverages*

Until 1963 Soviet national statistical handbooks published the data on annual ruble sales of alcoholic and nonalcoholic beverages in state retail trade. Unfortunately, starting with the 1963 handbook the sales of beverages have been concealed by adding them to sales of miscellaneous food products such as ice cream, coffee, cocoa, and various spices, and labeling this new category in trade statistics "other foods."

It is interesting to note that statistical handbooks for the republics do not follow the example of the national publication. In fact, almost all of the fifteen Soviet republics publish or conceal the data on sales of alcoholic beverages in their own ways. Some republics such as Kazakhstan, Latvia, and Turkmenistan continued to publish sales of alcoholic beverages, while others such as the Ukraine, Belorussia and Kirgizia lumped alcoholic beverages with miscellaneous foods. This "concealment by aggregation" was compounded in RSFSR trade statistics by lumping together the category "other foods" with the public dining markup. Nevertheless, some republican statistics are useful and will be utilized in this study.

The concealment is not very successful for the simple fact that the proverbial needle is much too large for the rather small haystack. Comparison of the sales data for the 1954–1962 period, for which we have separate sales data for beverages and miscellaneous foods, shows that the latter compose an almost constant ten percent of the combined sales. The available data for the sales of alcoholic beverages by republic suggest the same ratio with only minor fluctuations of ± 1.00 percent. Accordingly, the retail sales of alcoholic and nonalcoholic beverages for the USSR for the 1963–1977 period have been estimated by taking a constant 90 percent of published "other food" sales.

A major change in the composition of miscellaneous food sales in 1978 made the application of a constant adjustment factor of 90 percent unrealistic. In March of that year the retail price of coffee—one of the large components of miscellaneous foods—was raised from 4.50 to 20.00 rubles per kg [*Trud*, March 1, 1978, p. 3]. Such a significant change in the price of a major commodity must have affected the structure of the residual category.

Unfortunately, it is virtually impossible to estimate the changes brought about by the increase in coffee prices. As a first approximation we can proceed as follows. Between 1975 and 1978 the USSR imported on the average about 44,000 tons of coffee. Since the weight of coffee sold exceeds, slightly, the weight of imported coffee [Zotov 1958, p. 181], we will use 45,000 tons as our estimate of sales in 1978. Since coffee all but disappeared from stores in 1976–1977 [private communications] we can assume that the entire output was sold in 1978. The March increase in the price of coffee from 4.5 to 20 rubles per kg would have added about 600 million rubles to the sales of coffee. Thus, we will subtract this amount from total sales of "other foods" before applying the 90 percent adjustment.

Estimates of sales of nonalcoholic beverages are shown in column 3 of table 3.1. There are three broad groups of nonalcoholic beverages in the USSR: nonalcoholic beverages proper produced in various branches of the foods industry, bottled mineral waters, and carbonated sodas (not bottled) produced locally by trade organizations and vendors of the Ministry of Trade of the USSR.

Production, which in this case is equated with sales of the three groups in physical units, has been estimated on the basis of the following sources: *Promyshlennost'*

[1964, p. 455] for the 1955–1963 period; "Spirtovaia" [1965, p. 3] for 1964; Elagina et al., [1975, pp. 24–25] for 1965, 1970 and 1972; BSE [3rd ed., Vol. 19, p. 519] for 1973, and Burnasheva et al., [1977, pp. 30–32] for the 1975–1976 period. Estimates for the missing years have been made by interpolation.

The output of mineral water is reported in Soviet sources in bottles which have been converted to liters at 0.75 liters per bottle. The following output statistics were used to estimate the series: Zotov [1958, p. 129], and Denshchikov [1961, p. 8] for 1958 and 1960; Pykhov [1964, p. 7] for 1963; "Spirtovaia" [1965, p. 3] for 1964; Zotov, et al., [1967, p. 419] for 1965, and BSE [3rd ed., vol. 19, p. 519] for 1973. Estimates for the missing years were made by inter-and extra-polation. The output of carbonated sodas in the Ministry of Trade was reported at approximately 40 percent of industrial output of nonalcoholic beverages [Zotov et al., 1967, p. 419] and this percentage was applied for the entire period.

The sum of the three groups gives us the output of nonalcoholic beverages for the entire period. Using Fel'dman [1974, p. 36] data on the sale of nonalcoholic beverages in rubles for the 1965–1970 period we can calculate the average price per liter as 0.21 rubles in 1967 and 0.22 rubles thereafter. As a first approximation we will use an average price of 0.20 rubles per liter for the 1955–1964 period. The increase in price implied in Fel'dman reflects the introduction of fruit juices and other more expensive nonalcoholic beverages in the mid-1960s. We will assume that the trend continued and the average price reached 0.23 rubles per liter by 1976.

Subtraction of ruble sales of nonalcoholic beverages in column 3 of table 3.1 from ruble sales of all beverages in column 2 gives the estimates of rubles sales of alcoholic beverages only in column 4. Column 5 shows changes in stocks and inventories at the retail trade level as published in standard Soviet statistical sources. As was mentioned earlier, unfortunately no data are available on changes in stocks and inventories at wholesale level, in transit, or at producing enterprises.

Starting in 1976, Soviet national statistical handbooks *Narodnoe khoziaistvo SSSR* stopped publishing the data on retail trade inventories. Most regional statistical handbooks also discontinued this series but with some exceptions: the Ukraine, Belorussia, and the city of Moscow continued to publish retail trade inventory statistics through 1978. As a first approximation we can estimate the change in the national inventory levels on the basis of these three sources. Needless to say, these estimates are probably subject to a significant margin of error. On the other hand, no matter how uncertain these estimates are, they would be preferrable to an assumption of zero inventory change.

The estimates are made as follows. Changes in retail trade inventories in the Ukraine, Belorussia and Moscow amounted to −77 million rubles in 1976, +100 million rubles in 1977, and −70 million rubles in 1978. The share of inventories of alcoholic beverages of the three regional entities in 1975 was 20.5 percent of the national level. We will assume that the share remained constant and estimate the changes in the retail trade inventories for the USSR as:

1976 −380 million rubles
1977 +490 million rubles

Table 3.1. State retail trade in alcoholic beverages, million rubles

	Sales of "other foods"	Sales of all beverages	Sales of nonalcoholic beverages	Sales of alcoholic beverages	Changes in stocks	Total supply of alcoholic beverages
1955	8,192	7,261	309	6,952	−58	6,894
1956	8,419	7,460	313	7,147	109	7,256
1957	9,841	8,737	370	8,367	−51	8,316
1958	10,741	9,625	391	9,234	819	10,053
1959	11,306	10,059	445	9,614	63	9,677
1960	12,396	11,023	477	10,546	−393	10,153
1961	12,959	11,535	489	11,046	−232	10,814
1962	14,032	12,659	515	12,144	90	12,234
1963	14,914	13,423	542	12,881	197	13,078
1964	15,866	14,279	575	13,704	357	14,061
1965	17,290	15,561	617	14,944	304	15,248
1966	19,103	17,193	712	16,481	238	16,719
1967	21,354	19,219	785	18,434	−94	18,340
1968	23,064	20,758	844	19,914	−219	19,695
1969	24,812	22,331	900	21,431	168	21,599
1970	26,971	24,273	1,000	23,273	1,431	24,704
1971	29,141	26,227	1,045	25,182	809	25,991
1972	30,922	27,830	1,093	26,737	−831	26,406
1973	32,668	29,401	1,073	28,328	−534	27,794
1974	34,594	31,135	1,127	30,008	739	30,747
1975	37,009	33,308	1,200	32,108	136	32,244
1976	38,785	34,907	1,247	33,660	−380	33,280
1977	41,046	36,941	1,296	35,645	490	36,135
1978	42,809	38,528	1,347	37,181	−340	36,841
1979	44,958	40,462	1,400	39,062	n.a.	39,062

n.a.: Data are not available

1978 −340 million rubles
No republican data on inventory changes are available for 1979, and therefore a zero change must be recorded.

3.3. Prices of Vodka and Vodka-based Beverages

Vodka constitutes the bulk of sales in this commodity group although its share has been gradually decreasing from 94 percent in 1950 to some 80 percent in the early 1970s (see section 2.2). An accurate estimation of an average price of vodka-based beverages is almost impossible because of the large number of different types produced and the lack of data on the output mix. Thus, we will have to make some simplifying assumptions with respect to average prices of these beverages. The main determinant of the price of vodka-based beverages is alcohol content. For example, in 1974 the average price of 16 types of liqueurs available in Moscow was 6 rubles per liter with an average alcohol content of about 25 percent, while the average price of standard 40 percent vodkas was about 8.10 rubles [T33 8–74–KK].

We have earlier estimated the average alcohol content of vodka-based beverages in the early 1960s at some 30 percent. Using this percentage as a rough guide to price, we will estimate the latter at 4 rubles per liter. The following types of vodka were available in the USSR in the late 1950s and 1960s [Turgeon 1963, p. 112; Bush 1964, p. 10; Kornienko 1964, p. 88; Nazarian 1972, p. 24]: low quality 40% "Vodka," 4.50 rubles per liter; "Moscow special," 5.50 rubles per liter; "Stolichnaia," 6.14 rubles per liter. Using the output mix reported in Pykhov [1964, p. 6] we will then estimate the average price of one liter of vodka in the early 1960s at 5.10 rubles per liter. We will assume that this price was in effect from 1958 through 1965. As of January 1, 1958, prices of all alcoholic beverages were raised 21 percent [Malafeev 1964, p. 338; Turetskii, 1959, p. 436]. This would make the 1957 price 4.22 rubles per liter which agrees with an earlier CIA estimate of 4.24 [CIA 1963, p. 125] and the data provided by Chapman [1963, pp. 192–244].

Average prices in the 1965–1970 period were calculated by dividing sales data in rubles [Fel'dman 1972, p. 36], by our estimates of the supply of vodka in liters, as follows: 1965, 5.08 (rubles per liter); 1966, 5.24; 1967, 5.41; 1968, 5.53; 1969, 5.62; 1970, 5.71. According to these figures the average price of vodka and vodka products was increasing at a rate of about 2.4 percent per annum. There were no officially announced increases in vodka prices in these years, but the average price was growing because of up-grading of the output mix, i.e., substitution of more expensive brands for cheaper varieties. One well documented case of such disguised price increases was the withdrawal of the popular and high quality "Stolichnaia" vodka, priced at 6.14 rubles per liter, and its replacement by "Extra" vodka of the same quality but priced at 8.00 rubles per liter [Bush 1969, p. 8; Bush 1972, p. 8; Tiraspolsky 1974, pp. 79–123]. This process of "upgrading" the output mix continued throughout the 1970s. Thus, such brands as "Starka," "Moskovskaia," "Starorusskaia," and "Petrovskaia" were slowly disappearing to be replaced by "Pshenichnaia," "Sibirskaia," "Posol'skaia," "Belovezhskaia," "Kristall," all priced somewhat higher [T3T 8–80 LL].[2] Some of the vodkas withdrawn earlier, in fact reappeared later at a higher price; this happened, for instance, with "Stolichnaia" vodka which became again available in the late 1970s priced some 30–35 percent higher.

One factor supporting this observation is seen in the following. The higher quality Soviet vodkas are made with ethanol distilled from grain and potatoes, while ethanol distilled form sugar beets, molasses, or raw sugar is used for the production of lower quality vodkas and for fortification of wines. In the 1970–1975 period the share of ethanol produced from grains and potatoes rose from 36 to 66 percent of total ethanol produced from foodstuffs, thus providing the necessary inputs for expansion of production of higher quality vodkas.

With the exception of champagne and cognac there have been no officially announced increases in prices of alcoholic beverages in the 1970s, but all evidence indicates that in fact prices were rising both because of upgrading and because of official upward adjustments. In fact, a Soviet economist specializing in consumption, Lokshin, reported that in the 1969–1974 period, retail prices of cognac, champagne, and of some other strong alcoholic beverages were increased [1975, p. 57]. In Soviet terminology "strong alcoholic beverages" could mean only vodka and vodka-based products, and Lokshin must be referring to them.

Price indexes scattered in statistical sources also suggest that there were increases in prices of vodka and vodka-based products in the mid-1970s. National statistical sources and most republics have, unfortunately, stopped publishing vodka price indexes, substituting indexes for all alcoholic beverages. However, some republics such as the Ukraine, Moldavia, and Lithuania continued to publish vodka price indexes and these show small (1–2 percentage points) increases in 1973–74. The only price index for the vodka group for the entire USSR shows a 1.6 percent increase in the 1970–1975 period [Kostin 1980, p. 2a]. A Lithuanian statistical source gives separate price indexes for vodka and vodka-based beverages. The latter show an increase of 9.8 percent in 1973 and of 23.3 percent in 1974 (1970 = 100), while vodka proper is reported to have increased in price in 1974 by 0.1 percent.

It must be added that émigrés from the USSR have also reported increases in the price of vodka which were put into effect without official announcement [Radio Liberty files]. According to one such report, the price of vodka "Extra" was increased by 32 percent in December, 1973 [*Russkaia mysl'*, May 30, 1974]. As the price indexes cited above indicate, there must have been price increases in 1973–74, but unfortunately the reported rate of increase cannot be accepted as correct because we have evidence that "Extra" was selling in major Soviet cities at the same price in 1972 and in later years [T3T 8–74 KK, T3T 8–76 NN, T3T 2–76 EE]. We will estimate, based on this evidence, the year-by-year price index for vodka and vodka products as 1.02 for 1971 through 1979, with the exceptions of 1.03 for 1973 and 1.05 for 1976.

3.4. *Prices of Champagne*

In the 1960s popular brands of champagne were priced between 2.97 and 3.75 rubles per liter [Radio Liberty files; Bush 1964, p. 10; Turgeon 1963, p. 112]. We will use a simple average of 3.36 rubles per liter for the 1959–1969 period.

Champagne was included in the overall price increase of some 20 percent which went into effect on January 1, 1958, and was then rescinded on July 1, 1959. We will thus estimate the average pre-1958 price as 3.36 rubles, rising to 4.03 in 1958, and dropping to 3.66 in 1959. Western observers reported that champagne prices were raised by about 50 percent on July 1, 1970 [*Reuters* July 1, 1970; *Washington Post*, July 2, 1970]. A price index published in a recent Soviet source [Kostin 1980, p. 29] shows an increase of 28.2 percent in 1970 and of 20.9 percent thereafter. We will use these percentages to calculate the average 1970 price as 4.31 rubles and the average 1971 price as 5.21 rubles per liter. Western observers reported that most champagne brands were selling at about 6 rubles per liter in the 1974–1978 period (T3T 9–7 4KK, T3T 4–7 6EE). We will assume that the average price was increasing because of changes in the mix in favor of more expensive brands. As a first approximation, the average 1971 price will be increased by 2 percent per annum through the end of the period under consideration.

3.5. *Prices of Cognacs*

In 1958–1959 the prices of Soviet cognac varied from a low of 8.07 rubles per liter for a 40 percent three-star cognac to 12.24 rubles for a stronger five-star brand [Nazarian 1972, p. 24; Bush 1964, p. 10, and Bush 1967, p. 9]. As a first approximation we will assume an 80–20 ratio between the two brands, thus estimating the average price at 8.91 rubles per liter. We will use this price for the entire 1958–1969 period. In 1958 the price of cognac was increased by 20 percent and we can thus estimate the pre-1958 price as 7.43 rubles per liter. (The prices of all alcoholic beverages were raised by about 20 percent in 1958, but a year later the price increase for wines was rescinded. We will assume that the cut in prices did not affect cognacs.)

Western sources reported that prices of cognac were approximately doubled on July 1, 1970 [*Reuters*, July 1, 1970; *Washington Post*, July 2, 1970]. To reflect the mid-year price increase we will calculate the average 1970 price as 13.37 rubles per liter (see Kostin [1980, p. 29]) and the average 1971 price as 17.82 rubles per liter. In 1974–1979 Western observers reported cognac prices ranging from 16 to 32 rubles per liter in Moscow and Leningrad [Tiraspolsky 1974, pp. 79–123; T3T 9–74 KK, T3T 4–76 EE]. To reflect the probable change in the mix of cognacs in favor of more expensive ones and the growing imports, we will arbitrarily increase the average price by 1 percent per year in the 1972–1979 period.

3.6. *Prices of Beer*

The prices of various beers sold in the USSR remained almost unchanged during the period covered in this study; the average price of beer is affected primarily by changes in the output mix and such factors as changes in the proportion of draft and bottled beer sold. There are eight to ten brands of beer sold in the USSR, but Zhiguli beer constituted about 90 percent of all beer sold in this period [Zotov 1958, p. 125 and Kudriavtseva 1972, p. 58]. The price of Zhiguli beer is 0.43 rubles per liter of draft beer and 0.50 rubles per liter of bottled beer [Kudriavtseva 1972, p. 54]. Different zone prices were averaged using shares of beer produced by republics in 1975 as reported in Balashov [1979, p. 5]. The share of bottled beer rose from 32 percent in 1954 [Veselov and Shakhtan 1955, p. 60] to 53.5 percent in 1978 [Boiko 1979, p. 3]. Thus, based on these shares, the average price of Zhiguli beer rose from 0.45 rubles in 1954 to 0.47 in 1978. Judging from alcohol content [Veselov and Shakhtan 1955, p. 8] and other evidence, other brands of beer sold in the USSR are more expensive. The average price of all beer, estimated on the basis of data in Fel'dman [1972, p. 36], was 0.48 rubles in the 1965–1968 period, 0.49 in 1969, and 0.50 in 1970, which agrees with the evidence presented above. We will use 0.48 rubles per liter for the 1955–1968 period, and 0.50 for the 1970–1978 period.

3.7. *Prices of Grape Wines and Fruit and Berry Wines*

It is impossible to estimate average prices of grape and fruit wines without accurate information on individual prices by brands and of the output mix. There has been only one officially announced change in wine prices—a two-step increase in 1957–1958 of some 20 percent which was rescinded in 1959 [Stoliarov 1966, pp. 99–100]. However, the description of the alcohol content of Soviet wines indicates the output mix has been continuously changing in favor of stronger and more expensive fortified wines. Another factor which affects average prices of Soviet wines is the import of wines and the mix of imported wines. As was shown in the section on foreign trade, (1.8.) the import of wines fluctuated significantly over the years. For instance, in 1967 imported wines composed some 10 percent of domestic production, rising to 27 percent in 1970 and dropping again to 13 percent in 1977. Since the bulk of Soviet imports are inexpensive, low-alcohol-content dry wines from Algeria, Rumania and Bulgaria, rapid increases in imports would depress the average domestic price. Regional price differentials [Kudriavtseva 1972, pp. 62–68] and fluctuating yields of vineyards affecting output of wine of different republics also contribute to changes in average prices. Private communications from Western visitors to the USSR, which proved so helpful in the estimation of the prices of vodka, brandy, and other beverages, were of little utility because of the large number of brands and the absence of data on mix.

Under these circumstances, average prices of all Soviet wine (i.e., grape and fruit and berry wine) were estimated by the residual method. The previously estimated ruble sales of vodka, champagne, brandy, and beer were subtracted from the ruble value of total supply of alcoholic beverages in the given year (table 3.1). The ruble sales of wine thus calculated were then divided by domestic supply of grape, and fruit and berry wine (table 1.4). Average prices of wine estimated in this manner appear to be reasonable and agree roughly with indirect evidence such as changes in the output mix, alcohol content, and imports.

Estimates of separate prices of grape and fruit and berry wine are needed for subsequent analysis. Thus, imperfect as they might be, they were made as follows. According to Kudriavtseva [1972, p. 68] an average post-1967 reform wholesale price of 13 types of fruit and berry wines produced in the RSFSR was 0.59 rubles per liter. Turnover tax rates on fruit and berry wines averaged some 56 percent of retail price of fruit wines in 1965 [Klemenchuk and Popov 1967, p. 79]; we will roughly adjust this rate down to 50 percent to reflect changes in costs and wholesale prices affected in the 1967 price reform. The retail trade markup on fruit and berry wines was 7 percent [Bakanov 1968, p. 167]. Using these three elements we can estimate the average retail price of fruit and berry wines in 1967 as 1.37 rubles per liter.

Having previously estimated the average retail price of all wine as 2.05 rubles per liter, and knowing the separate supply figures for grape and fruit wines, we can

Table 3.2. Prices of alcoholic beverages, by type, rubles per liter*

	Vodka	Grape wine	Fruit & berry wines	Champagne	Cognac	Beer
1955	4.22	1.67	1.00	3.36	7.43	0.48
1956	4.22	1.69	1.01	3.36	7.43	0.48
1957	4.22	2.05	1.23	3.36	7.43	0.48
1958	5.10	2.05	1.23	4.03	8.91	0.48
1959	5.10	1.73	1.04	3.66	8.91	0.48
1960	5.10	1.83	1.10	3.36	8.91	0.48
1961	5.10	1.84	1.12	3.36	8.91	0.48
1962	5.10	2.03	1.22	3.36	8.91	0.48
1963	5.10	2.07	1.24	3.36	8.91	0.48
1964	5.10	2.26	1.35	3.36	8.91	0.48
1965	5.08	2.36	1.42	3.36	8.91	0.48
1966	5.24	2.33	1.40	3.36	8.91	0.48
1967	5.41	2.21	1.33	3.36	8.91	0.48
1968	5.53	2.08	1.25	3.36	8.91	0.48
1969	5.66	1.96	1.17	3.36	8.91	0.49
1970	5.71	2.23	1.34	4.31	13.37	0.50
1971	5.82	2.35	1.41	5.21	17.82	0.50
1972	5.94	2.38	1.43	5.31	18.00	0.50
1973	6.12	2.55	1.53	5.42	18.18	0.50
1974	6.43	2.38	1.44	5.53	18.36	0.50
1975	6.56	2.16	1.30	5.64	18.54	0.50
1976	6.69	2.08	1.25	5.75	18.73	0.50
1977	6.83	2.52	1.51	5.87	18.92	0.50
1978	6.97	2.71	1.63	5.98	19.10	0.50
1979	7.11	2.63	1.57	6.10	19.29	0.50

*Without the cost of the bottle.

now estimate the average price of grape wine alone as 2.22 rubles per liter. Thus, the average price of fruit and berry wine was 60 percent of the price of grape wine. Assuming, in the absence of any additional data, that this ratio remained constant during the entire period under study, separate grape and fruit wine prices were calculated. Prices so estimated are definitely not as accurate as average prices of all wines. One of the obvious shortcomings of this method is that the impact of imports of inexpensive wines carries through to the prices of fruit and berry wines, which should not have been affected. In the absence of additional data this was, unfortunately, the only possible method to use.

3.8. Price Indexes for Alcoholic Beverages

Official Soviet consumer price indexes are notoriously bad. They are constructed on the basis of a small and fixed sample of consumer goods and thus do not capture the introduction of new or modified products at higher prices. Therefore only officially declared changes in prices of products in the sample will be

Table 3.3. Sales of alcoholic beverages by type, current prices, million rubles

	Total	Vodka	Wine total	Wine grape	Wine fruit	Champagne	Cognac	Beer
1955	6,894	4,916	899	770	130	66	126	887
1956	7,256	5,165	1,030	875	153	74	119	868
1957	8,316	5,912	1,291	1,144	189	80	89	944
1958	10,053	7,405	1,471	1,265	208	105	107	963
1959	9,677	6,992	1,337	1,144	192	102	122	1,124
1960	10,153	7,053	1,656	1,435	223	100	134	1,210
1961	10,814	7,441	1,813	1,564	249	108	159	1,293
1962	12,234	8,252	2,315	2,026	296	119	183	1,365
1963	13,078	8,609	2,780	2,449	329	126	208	1,355
1964	14,061	9,012	3,321	2,933	393	137	225	1,366
1965	15,248	9,616	3,710	3,271	452	150	242	1,530
1966	16,719	10,412	4,221	3,765	457	163	259	1,664
1967	18,340	11,558	4,588	4,119	466	180	266	1,748
1968	19,695	12,542	4,786	4,279	513	196	321	1,850
1969	21,599	13,493	5,550	5,037	530	213	388	1,955
1970	24,704	13,755	7,841	7,143	683	299	703	2,106
1971	25,991	13,648	8,752	7,917	835	389	984	2,218
1972	26,406	13,217	9,358	8,347	1,011	427	1,042	2,362
1973	27,794	15,153	8,353	6,653	1,700	469	1,264	2,555
1974	30,747	16,216	9,931	7,771	2,160	515	1,368	2,717
1975	32,244	17,279	9,932	7,852	2,080	588	1,569	2,876
1976	33,280	17,896	10,282	7,767	2,515	648	1,465	2,989
1977	36,135	18,776	12,069	8,898	3,130	710	1,449	3,131
1978	36,841	19,906	11,461	7,875	3,586	777	1,455	3,242
1979	39,062	20,278	13,235	9,560	3,675	848	1,500	3,201

reflected in price indexes. Such price indexes, accordingly, understate price increases. The degree of the bias of the consumer price indexes depends, of course, on the nature of the product—for branches in which the introduction of new products is slow (meat products, bakery goods) the bias will not be as pronounced as in branches where new products appear regularly. The downward bias in alcoholic beverage price indexes is probably particularly strong because of the continuous upgrading of the product mix which was discussed above.

Official Soviet statistical sources published a price index for vodka and vodka-based beverages until 1969. Starting with 1970, a price index for all alcoholic beverages was substituted for the vodka index. The official price index for alcoholic beverages for 1979 was 1.03 (1970 = 1.00).

It will be noted that Soviet indexes of the sales of consumer goods in constant prices are derived by deflating the sales measured in current prices by the official price index. Since price indexes understate price increases, the sales indexes obtained this way will overstate the real increases in sales. This can be clearly seen in the case of alcoholic beverages where the official sales index for 1979 was 4.97 (1955 = 1.00), implying that per capita real consumption increased 3.7 times (based

Table 3.4. Price indexes for all alcoholic beverages (1955 = 100)

1955	1.00	1964	1.220	1973	1.450
1956	1.00	1965	1.230	1974	1.467
1957	1.060	1966	1.252	1975	1.452
1958	1.206	1967	1.257	1976	1.468
1959	1.147	1968	1.260	1977	1.551
1960	1.159	1969	1.260	1978	1.598
1961	1.160	1970	1.324	1979	1.603
1962	1.189	1971	1.371		
1963	1.193	1972	1.400		

on a population increase of 1.34), an impossibly high number.

The use of notoriously biased price indexes is probably justified by Soviet statistical authorities by the fact that the overall picture of consumer welfare in the USSR as reflected in consumer goods sales in constant prices produced by this method is a favorable one. However, in the case of alcoholic beverages, the price index which understates price increases and overstates sales presents a picture of unrealistically high growth in drinking. A price index for all alcoholic beverages based on prices estimated in table 3.2 and using 1965 expenditures as weights is shown in table 3.4.

It should be noted that in September 1981 Soviet authorities announced increases in prices of alcoholic beverages ranging from 17 to 27 percent [*Pravda*, September 15, 1981, p. 3]. New prices of individual beverages were not included in the announcement, but according to some reports the price of a standard vodka was raised 20 percent [*Chicago Tribune*, October 1, 1981, p. 3] and the price of "Russkaia" vodka was raised 17 percent [T3T1–82BF]. Increases in wine prices were probably around 25 percent.

The across-the-board increase in prices of all alcoholic beverages in 1958 and increases in prices of selected beverages in the early 1970s were clearly intended by authorities as antidrinking measures and were introduced in conjunction with antidrinking campaigns. In contrast the September 1981 increases in prices of alcoholic beverages did not coincide with any special antidrinking decree or announcement and were a part of a general price increase for a number of major commodity groups such as jewelry, gasoline, furniture, furs, carpets, china, and tobacco products. In all probability these price increases can be explained as a measure to reduce cash holdings of the population and to restore the balance between consumer expenditures and incomes.

The advisability of the inclusion of alcoholic beverages in a general price increase can be seriously questioned. In all probability it will be harmful in the long run because at least some Soviet drinkers will turn to samogon and other homemade beverages, alcohol surrogates, and to drinking stolen toxic industrial alcohol. The fact that the announced price increases cover both vodka and wines and that price ratios were changed in favor of vodka[3] is somewhat puzzling, particularly as it came so soon after the 1979 45 percent increase in the price of beer sold in restaurants. Soviet authorities have long established a goal of reducing the share of vodka and other strong beverages in the total consumption of alcohol and of increasing the shares of wines and beer. And, as shown in table 2.5, they have been fairly successful in the pursuit of this goal, with the share of strong beverages declining from 76 percent in 1955 to 48 percent in 1979. The 1981 price changes may very well reverse this trend.

3.9. *Turnover Taxes on Alcoholic Beverages and Budgetary Revenues*

The Soviet fiscal system is characterized by moderately progressive small income taxes and very high excise taxes differentiated by commodities. The rates of the excise tax, termed the turnover tax, on alcoholic beverages are among the highest; among commodities being taxed turnover tax revenues collected on sales of alcoholic beverages account for between 10 and 11 percent of all state revenues in the USSR.

Soviet sources seldom publish turnover tax rates or absolute ruble amounts of taxes collected on alcoholic beverages. As with other commodities, tax rates on alcoholic beverages are highly differentiated by type, brand, buyer, and even by such factors as administrative subordination of the producing enterprise. Thus, for instance, in the RSFSR the tax rate on beer produced in enterprises of local (*raion* — a small administrative area) subordination is 50 percent while the rate on beer produced on republican enterprises is 72 percent [Klemenchuk and Popov, 1967, p. 79]. At the same time there is a certain measure of overall stability of rates. Thus, the tax rate on vodka ranged from 83.0 to 91.0 percent of retail price in the 1930s [Davies 1958, p. 288; Holzman 1962, p. 144] and was reported as 88.4 percent in 1967 [Nazarian 1972, p. 24]. In the 1972–1975 period, tax revenues on alcoholic beverages amounted to an almost constant 35 percent of total turnover tax collections [Sorokin et al., eds., 1977, p. 119]. The main purpose of this section is to establish the overall magnitude of tax collections on alcoholic beverages, and taxes on specific groups of products are of no importance. Because of this and the observed relative stability of tax rates, the estimates made in this section will be based on more tenuous assumptions and will avoid minute details included in the analysis in other sections of this study.

Vodka and Vodka-based Beverages. The rate of 88.4 percent of retail price of vodka cited in Nazarian [1972, p. 24] will be applied to the entire group of vodka and vodka-based beverages and will be used for the 1967–1979 period. In the 1967 price reform the retail trade markup on vodka was increased 4 to 4.8 percent and, since retail prices were not affected, the change was compensated for in the tax rate [Bakanov 1968, p. 167]. We will thus roughly estimate the tax rate as 89.2 percent for the pre-1967 period. The 20 percent increase in the price of vodka introduced in 1958 was made without any changes in wholesale prices and thus affected the turnover tax rate only. The pre-1958 tax rate is then estimated as 0.886.

*Wine Group.*The wine group, which includes grape and fruit wines and cognac, is taxed depending on alcohol and sugar content of beverages and a number of other factors, including the location of producers. The rates range from a low of 16.5 percent on dry table wines to a high of 52.5 percent on fortified wines [Nazarian 1972, p. 24]. Under the circumstances, the estimation of tax payments on individual brands would be impossible and we will use approximate rates for the entire group. The average rate was reported as 57.7 percent in 1964 [Kondrashev and Kondrashov 1969, p. 29]. Assuming that the rate was reported in the usual Soviet manner as related to retail price less retail and wholesale trade markups, we will adjust the rate down to about 54 percent of retail price based on known markups [Bakanov 1968, p. 167]. In the 1966–67 price reform the markup rates as well as wholesale prices on wine were raised without adjustments in retail prices [Kudriavtseva 1972, pp. 62–69], and we will change the average rate down to 46 percent to reflect these changes. Data available in Sorokin et al., eds. [1977, p. 119] and our estimates of wine sales yield average rates ranging from 44 to 48 percent in the 1972–1975 period, confirming the accuracy of the estimated 46 percent rate. This rate will then be used for the entire post-1965 period. As was reported above, the prices of wines were raised 20 percent in 1958, but the measure was rescinded in mid-1959. As in the case of vodka, there is no evidence of corresponding adjustments in wholesale prices or trade markups in this period, and the price changes would have affected only the tax rates which were then estimated as 54 percent in the 1955–57 period, 62 percent in 1958, and 58 percent in 1959.

Beer. In 1965 the turnover tax rate on beer was reported to average 65.8 percent of retail price net of retail and wholesale markups [Klemenchuk and Popov 1967, pp. 76, 79]. The retail trade markup in the 1960s was 9.5 percent [Bakanov 1968, p. 167]. The wholesale markup on beer is not known, but generally the ratio of retail to wholesale markup is about 5:1 [Birman 1970, pp. 169–177] and we can take it to be about 2 percent of retail price. Accordingly, the turnover tax rate applicable to retail price without netting out trade markups would be about 58 percent. In the absence of any additional information we will use this rate for the 1955–1966 period.

Enterprise prices of beer were raised 10 percent by January 1, 1967, and again 2.3 percent on January 1, 1968 [Kudriavtseva 1972, pp. 59–60]; the retail trade markup was raised to 12 percent [Bakanov 1968, p. 167]. Since retail prices of beer were not affected by the 1967 reform we can estimate that the turnover tax rate was reduced to about 53 percent of retail price. We will use this rate for the 1967–1978 period, table 3.5 summarizes turnover tax revenues collected on all alcoholic beverages sold in retail trade.

Turnover taxes on alcoholic beverages contribute in a significant way to the taxation burden in the USSR. In 1979 Soviet citizens paid about 88 billion rubles of taxes consisting of 23 billion rubles of income taxes and some 65 billion taxes in turnover taxes on consumer goods.[4] Thus, taxes of 25.4 billion rubles on alcoholic beverages made up about 29 percent of the total taxes paid by the population. Simi-

Table 3.5. Turnover tax collections on sales of alcoholic beverages, millions of rubles

1955	5,459	1964	10,895	1973	19,916
1956	5,739	1965	11,603	1974	19,389
1957	6,574	1966	12,305	1975	21,209
1958	8,149	1967	13,459	1976	22,443
1959	7,738	1968	14,507	1977	23,168
1960	8,852	1969	15,793	1978	24,820
1961	8,534	1970	17,343	1979	25,416
1962	9,605	1971	17,898		
1963	10,202	1972	17,916		

Table 3.6. Taxes on alcoholic beverages, tax per liter of pure alcohol, rubles

	1955	1967	1979
Strong beverages of 40 percent alcohol and higher (vodka and cognac)	9.46	12.10	16.94
Other beverages (wines and beer)	6.68	6.19	4.96

lar calculations show that this ratio had been about the same in earlier years.

There have been significant changes in the structure of turnover taxes on alcoholic beverages. Since early 1955, the Soviet authorities have been trying to encourage consumption of wines and beer and to reduce the share of strong distilled spirits. This policy is reflected in taxes levied on different beverages as shown in table 3.6 below (estimated on the basis of data in tables 2.5 and 3.5).

The absolute magnitude of the tax burden per capita, therefore, depends to a large degree on the mix of beverages being consumed.

Using the regional consumption for 1967 (table 6.3) we can calculate the overall alcohol turnover 1967 tax payments (rubles) per person fifteen years and older as follows: RSFSR, 93.49; Turkmenistan, Tadzhikistan, Uzbekistan, and Kirgizia, 40.63; Armenia, Georgia, Azerbaidzhan, 36.14.

As the result of further increases in tax rates on strong beverages and cuts in tax rates on beer and wines, by 1979 regional tax differentials had significantly increased but accurate estimates are impossible.

The turnover tax on alcoholic beverages is by far the most important source of state revenues in the USSR, although its relative share is gradually declining. During the period of this study, taxes on alcoholic beverages constituted about 11.5 percent of all state revenues in 1965; this share dropped to about 9.7 percent in 1975 and 9.0 percent in 1979. It should be noted, however, that the downward trend was reversed in 1981 when the government announced increases in retail prices of alcoholic beverages ranging from 17 to 27 percent (*Pravda*, September 15, 1981, p. 3). Since no adjustments in wholesale prices or in trade markups were announced, we can assume that the reported increases in retail prices were achieved by corresponding upward adjustments in turnover tax rates. Accurate data are not available, but in all probability demand for alcoholic beverages in the USSR is relatively inelastic [Riabushkin 1966, p. 228; Beliaevskii et al., eds., 1968, p. 156], and the sales should not be seriously affected by price increases. The share of turnover taxes on alcoholic beverages in the state budget will probably grow then to some 12–13 percent by 1982.

Revenues derived by the state budget from production and sale of alcoholic beverages are not restricted to turnover tax collections: they include deductions from profits and revenues earned by foreign trade operations. Accurate calculations are difficult if not impossible, but rough estimates suggest that in 1975 payments into the state budget, which were based on deductions from profits earned by alcohol and alcoholic beverage industries, amounted to some 900 million rubles and that deductions from profits of trade and public dining organizations yielded another 500 million rubles.

Profits of alcohol and alcoholic beverage industries were estimated as follows. Soviet statistical sources regularly publish total profit of the food industry, and profits of its four major components, i.e. sugar, meat, fish, and dairy industries. The residual which is equal to about one-half of total food industry profits was distributed among branches for which profit data are not available proportionally to the value of fixed capital stock. The latter statistics were reported for 1970 in Vinogradov [1976, p 766] and, in all probability, did not change much by 1975. In 1975, Soviet industry on the average, turned over to the state budget 57 percent of the profit and this average rate was applied to the estimated profits of the alcohol and alcoholic beverage industries. Profits in retail and wholesale trade and in public dining, which were reported regularly in Soviet statistical sources, were distributed proportionally to sales. Deductions from profits of all state enterprises were 56 percent in 1975 and this ratio was applied to the estimated profits derived from sale of alcoholic beverages.

In the late 1970s net imports of alcoholic beverages (export minus imports) averaged annually some 400 million rubles. Without going into details of Soviet accounting of foreign trade operations, we should simply note that imports of most products, particularly consumer goods, are highly profitable because prices paid by domestic buyers of imported goods exceed prices paid by importing agencies by a significant margin. For instance in 1975 cognac, which was bought in foreign markets for about 2 rubles per liter, was selling, net of turnover taxes, for about 10 rubles in retail trade; imported wines were purchased abroad at prices ranging from 0.14 to 0.90 rubles per liter and then sold to Soviet buyers for about 1.20 rubles. Accordingly, net imports which cost some 400 million rubles to buy abroad would sell domestically for three to four times this amount with the difference termed "special earnings of foreign trade" paid into the state treasury.[5]

It should be noted that there are also some budgetary subsidies to the alcohol industry, but they are insignificant compared with budgetary revenues. For instance, agricultural producers receive a fixed price of 60 rubles per ton of potatoes

Table 3.7. Share of alcoholic beverages sold through public dining facilities, 1955-1963

1955	24%	1958	18%	1961	15%
1956	24	1959	15	1962	15
1957	20	1960	16	1963	15

delivered to ethanol plants for processing, but the plants pay only 40 rubles with the difference of 20 rubles covered out of the state budget [Pal'chuk 1978, p. 85]. Since 1965 the Soviet ethanol industry has been using about 2 million tons of potatoes annually (see table 4.4), and thus the subsidy from the state budget amounts to some 40 million rubles. In certain years small budgetary subsidies may have been paid to plants processing grains, although there are no direct references to this practice in literature. These subsidies are thus quite modest and can be safely disregarded when we look at the billions of rubles of budgetary revenues derived from the alcohol and alcoholic beverage industries.

Addition of deductions from profits and of special earnings from foreign trade operations to turnover tax collections would thus increase the share of revenues from alcohol in total state revenues by one to two percentage points. No other industry or economic activity in the USSR comes even close to the alcohol industry in terms of contributions to the state budget. State revenues from production and sales of alcoholic beverages are therefore such an important factor in the administration of fiscal policy in the USSR that it is difficult to imagine that it would not frustrate or at least constrain any government antidrinking measures and policies.[6]

3.10. *Sales of Alcoholic Beverages Through Public Dining Facilities*

In earlier sections, sales of alcoholic beverages in value terms were measured in state-fixed retail prices, i.e., prices actually paid by Soviet buyers of beverages in stores. A significant share of beverages is, however, sold in restaurants, cafes, railroad club cars, and other public eating places, collectively known in Soviet trade literature as "public dining." To cover the additional costs of preparing and serving meals and beverages, the public dining facilities charge prices which consist of state retail prices plus special supplements, or "nadbavki." The standard practice in Soviet statistical sources is to record sales of all food products measured in retail prices and to list separately the sum of all supplements collected in public dining.

The task of this section is, therefore, to estimate the sum of supplements collected on sales of alcoholic beverages in public dining facilities. The estimation is possible only with a significant margin of error, because of the absence of detailed data on the mix of beverages in public dining and public dining markups. However, the importance of this section in the framework of the entire study is only marginal and the estimates needed only for overall budgetary analysis.

The ruble value of the markup on alcoholic beverages will be estimated in several steps. Soviet standard statistical sources reported the percentage share of alco-

Table 3.8. Share of alcoholic beverages sold through
public dining facilities, 1964-1979

1964	15%	1970	12.5%	1976	9%
1965	15	1971	10	1977	9
1966	15	1972	9	1978	9
1967	15	1973	9	1979	9
1968	15	1974	9		
1969	15	1975	9		

holic beverages sold through public dining facilities for the 1955–1963 period as in
table 3.7.

Using the data offered in Bychkov [1978, p. 104] we can estimate the share of
alcoholic beverages consumed in public dining as 10 percent in 1971 and 9 percent
in 1975. Fragmentary data available for some republics and for the city of Moscow
suggest that the share was relatively stable in the 1960s and dropped sharply in
1970–71. The explanation for the drop probably lies in the significant increase in
the prices of vodka and some other beverages served in public dining facilities in
February 1970 [*New York Times*, February 24, 1970, p. 4; *Reuters*, July 1, 1970;
Radio Liberty files].

Using the Bychkov rates given above we will roughly estimate the shares in table
3.8. The rate of the markup on beer is about 10 percent of the sales price [Bychkov
1978, p. 103]. One adjustment to the estimated value of the markup on beer had to
be made: On July 1, 1979, the price of beer sold in public dining was increased by
45% [*Pravda* July 1, 1979, p. 3] implying a boost in the markup rate to 38%. This
increase is reflected in the markup data for 1979.

The rates of the markup on vodka, wines, and other alcoholic beverages are too
complex to estimate, particularly without detailed information on the mix of beverages sold in public dining. The average rate on all beverages except beer was about
20 percent in 1966 [Volkov 1968, p. 728] and 30 percent in 1974 [Lokshin 1975, p.
10]. The increase in the average markup probably occurred early in 1970 as was discussed above. Thus, as a first approximation we will use the rate of 20 percent for
the 1955–1969 period and 30 percent for the 1970–1979 period. The share of beer
sold in public dining in the 1970s was about 45 percent [Bychkov 1978, p. 104] and
we will use this rate for the entire period.

The estimation of the markup in public dining was then made as follows. The
percentage rates were applied to total sales of alcoholic beverages given in table 3.1
to obtain the ruble value of alcoholic beverages sold through public dining. The
markup on beer sold in public dining was estimated by applying a constant 10 percent rate to the value of beer sold (45 percent of beer sales estimated in table 3.3).
Subtracting the value of beer sold from the value of sales of all alcoholic beverages,
and applying a 20 percent rate for 1955–1969 and a 30 percent rate for 1970–1979,
gives us the ruble value of markup on all other alcoholic beverages. Summing up
the markup on beer and on other alcoholic beverages gives us the total markup.

Table 3.9. Markup on alcoholic beverages
sold in public dining, million rubles

	Total markup	Urban markup	Rural markup
1955	294	238	56
1956	304	246	58
1957	293	240	53
1958	289	240	49
1959	238	202	36
1960	283	241	42
1961	284	244	40
1962	303	264	39
1963	325	283	42
1964	350	305	45
1965	380	331	49
1966	420	370	50
1967	475	418	57
1968	514	452	62
1969	585	515	70
1970	668	588	80
1971	556	489	67
1972	589	518	71
1973	535	471	64
1974	565	497	68
1975	608	541	67
1976	640	570	70
1977	881	775	106
1978	712	627	85
1979	964	848	116

We can also roughly estimate the value of markup on alcoholic beverages in
urban and rural areas, on the basis of percentage distribution regularly reported in
Soviet statistical sources. This method will probably generate some error because
the reported percentages are based on total sales in public dining facilities in urban
and rural areas, and we are thus assuming that the markup on alcoholic beverages
is proportional to total sales. Unfortunately, this is the only possible method that
can be used. These estimates are presented in table 3.9.

4. Production and use of Ethanol

4.1 *Production*

Chemically pure ethanol (C_2H_5OH) would be too expensive to produce industrially, and the various types of ethanol manufactured in the USSR differ, depending on the level and the chemical nature of alien elements such as aldehydes, fusel oils, ethers, and other compound alcohols. The chemical composition of these impurities depends primarily on the raw material used in the production of ethanol. The various ethanols produced in the USSR can be classified according to the raw materials from which they were derived into two broad classes: food-based and synthetic ethanols. The former can be derived from virtually all agricultural crops, but in practice they are produced from grain, potatoes, sugar beets, molasses, and sugar. The synthetic ethanols can be broadly grouped into three types: synthetic ethanol proper, derived from the ethylene in the petroleum and gas industry; the sulfite ethanol, produced from paper and pulp; and the so-called hydrolytic ethanol, derived by the process of hydrolysis of wood and other fibrous matters [Khalaim 1972, pp. 119–123; Bachurin and Smirnov 1975, pp. 20–21; and Stabnikov et al., 1976, pp. 258–263]. A certain quantity of ethanol is produced in the USSR from fermented grapes, fruits, and berries in the wine industry, but this section will not be concerned with it. The production of food-based and synthetic ethanol is summarized in table 4.1.

The data are from standard Soviet statistical yearbooks supplemented by the following sources: Zotov[1958, p. 110]; "Spirtovaia"[1965, p. 1]; Pykhov[1966, p. 17 and p. 29]; Pykhov [1973, p. 17 and p. 31]; BSE [3rd ed., Vol. 24, p. 324]; Rudavka and Nichik[1976, p. 31]; and *Vestnik statistiki*[No. 10, 1980, p. 79]. The output data had to be estimated for synthetic ethanol for the years 1971–1979, and for food-based alcohol for the years 1976–1979. As the first step, total (synthetic and food) output series for 1971–1975 were estimated on the basis of published production statistics available for the RSFSR, the Ukraine, Belorussia, Latvia, Estonia, and Azerbaidzhan. In the 1970s these six republics produced over 95 percent of the ethanol in the USSR, and thus the estimates are fairly reliable. The output of synthetic ethanol was then estimated by subtracting the available output statistics for food-based ethanol from the estimated totals. The least reliable are the figures for synthetic and food-based ethanol produced in the 1976–1979 period, which were roughly estimated on the basis of published output indexes[1] and some fragmentary data for production by republics. The decline in the output level of both the synthetic and the food-based ethanol in 1978–1979 is not surprising and reflects poor agricultural harvests and a reduction of synthetic alcohol production in Azerbaidzhan.

Production of synthetic ethanol broken down by types is of only marginal interest in this study and, therefore, only selected years are shown in Table 4.2. The

Table 4.1. Production of raw food-based and synthetic ethanol, million liters

	Total ethanol produced	Synthetic (nonfood) ethanol	Ethanol from foodstuffs
1955	1,277	200	1,077
1956	1,288	256	1,032
1957	1,572	327	1,245
1958	1,639	479	1,160
1959	1,690	588	1,101
1960	1,707	654	1,053
1961	1,840	670	1,170
1962	2,037	714	1,323
1963	1,966	804	1,162
1964	2,131	1,019	1,112
1965	2,360	1,073	1,287
1966	2,430	1,096	1,334
1967	2,626	1,180	1,446
1968	2,670	1,171	1,499
1969	2,730	1,185	1,546
1970	2,796	1,215	1,581
1971	2,746	1,234	1,512
1972	2,754	1,254	1,500
1973	2,953	1,306	1,647
1974	3,171	1,331	1,840
1975	3,130	1,333	1,797
1976	3,193	1,373	1,820
1977	3,280	1,420	1,860
1978	3,240	1,400	1,840
1979	3,120	1,370	1,750

series are based on Denis'ev and Ognev [1958, p. 15], Pykhov [1966, p. 20] Pykhov [1973, p. 20], BSE [3rd ed., Vol. 6, p. 487], "Desiataia" [1976, pp. 1–2], and Kropotov [1968, p. 1].

4.2 Use of Agricultural Commodities in the Production of Ethanol

Food-based ethanol is produced from a variety of agricultural commodities such as different grains (wheat, corn, rye, barley), potatoes, molasses, sugar beets, and raw sugar. Industrial production of chemically pure ethanol is impossible because small quantities of various chemicals are always present in the finished product. The nature, level, and mix of these impurities is mainly dependent on the commodity used in distillation. In Russia and Eastern Europe grain ethanol is held traditionally to be the best for human consumption, both because the level of impurities is somewhat lower and because its taste is not unpleasant. Potato-based ethanol is considered to be almost as good. According to Soviet state quality standards, the best ethanol, labelled "Extra," is produced only from grains [Stabnikov et al., 1976,

Table 4.2. Production of synthetic ethanol by types, selected years, millions of liters

Year	Total synthetic ethanol	Ethylene-based (oil & gas) ethanol	Sulfite ethanol (paper & pulp)	Hydrolytic ethanol (wood)
1955	200	53	59	88
1958	479	265	89	125
1960	654	413	98	143
1968	1,171	852	125	194
1970	1,215	897	128	190
1975	1,333	1,034	137	162

p. 259] and better quality vodkas are produced from "Extra" ethanol.

Ethanol produced from sugary commodities such as molasses and sugar beets is considered inferior because of its unpleasant taste and odor. In fact, in Tsarist times vodka was produced only from grain or potato-based ethanol, and small quantities of ethanol produced from molasses were used for industrial purposes or for export [Vol'shanskii et al., 1977, p. 42; BSE, 1st ed., Vol. 11, p. 132]. In the Soviet period, the rapid growth of demand for ethanol for human consumption and for industrial purposes, combined with the lagging supply of grains and potatoes, led to an increase in the use of molasses in the production of ethanol. The share of ethanol produced from molasses rose from 6 percent in 1913 to 20 percent by 1938 [Pykhov 1973, p. 15]. In all probability the inferior molasses-based ethanol was mainly used for industrial purposes. However, by the early 1950s some molasses-based ethanol was already used in the production of vodka and in wine making.

The introduction of sugar beets and, several years later, of raw sugar, into the production of ethanol requires an explanation. In the late 1950s the USSR significantly expanded sugar beet production and sugar refining capacities. Growing commercial relations with Cuba and contracted imports of large quantities of Cuban raw sugar soon led to surpluses of sugar beets and to excess capacities in sugar refineries. The growing demand for ethanol to produce alcoholic beverages and for industrial purposes could not be easily satisfied by traditional agricultural inputs such as grains and potatoes, and in the early 1960s the industry began processing sugar beets into ethanol. The supply of sugar, however, continued to outstrip the demand: in 1962, for instance, the stocks of sugar in industry and trade reached some 4.8 million tons, compared with an output of 7.8 million tons that year. The government would have liked to increase the per capita consumption of sugar, but one obvious way of doing this—a cut in prices—was unacceptable, because it would lead to a higher use of sugar in domestic moonshine production of alcoholic beverages. Facing the growing stocks of sugar, Soviet industry started to divert a part of supplies to the production of ethanol.

The use of sugar beets and of sugar in the production of ethanol is inefficient in terms of existing procurement prices and it is wasteful of resources. Also, as was pointed out earlier, the ethanol produced is of inferior quality with an unpleasant

Table 4.3. Distribution of total food-based ethanol by type of agricultural inputs used in production, percent

	Potatoes	Grain	Molasses	Sugar beets	Sugar
1955	13.0	65.4	21.5	0.1	0
1956	17.6	45.0	37.4	0	0
1957	n.a.	n.a.	n.a.	0	0
1958				0	
1959				0	
1960	6.8	40.4	50.7	2.1	0
1961	13.0	34.0	53.0	0	0
1962	3.6	26.8	42.2	6.3	21.2
1963	6.1	27.1	41.8	3.9	23.1
1964	15.0	37.3	43.6	3.8	0.3
1965	20.6	16.9	52.0	6.4	4.1
1966	15.4	10.9	47.2	6.3	20.2
1967	13.7	20.3	43.3	5.7	17.0
1968	18.3	19.4	46.2	4.7	11.4
1969	15.4	21.2	47.3	3.2	12.9
1970	12.6	23.4	34.9	2.9	26.2
1971	11.6	36.3	43.3	2.8	6.0
1972					
1973	11.7	49.0	39.2	neg.	neg.
1974					
1975	11.6	53.9	34.5	0	26.2
1976	n.a.	n.a.	32.0	n.a.	n.a.
1977	n.a.	n.a.	34.5	n.a.	n.a.
1978	n.a.	n.a.	n.a.	n.a.	n.a.
1979	n.a.	n.a.	n.a.	n.a.	n.a.

n.a.: Data are not available
neg.: Negligible

odor. Initially, it was described as a temporary solution [Pykhov 1973, p. 31], but as can be seen from the data in table 4.3, the practice continued well into the 1970s.

The use of sugar for ethanol production is an embarrassment to the government because of its obvious inefficiency and its political implications. Thus, in earlier Soviet sources the use of sugar was disguised by terms such as "other raw materials" [Pykhov 1966, p. 26; Klemenchuk and Popov 1967, p. 6]. But in later publications the use of sugar was openly recognized [Khalaim, 1972, p. 21; Pykhov 1973, p. 31]. Tables 4.3 and 4.4 show tabulations on the use of agricultural inputs in the production of ethanol. The data are from Zotov [1958, p. 189], Pykhov [1964, p. 4], Pykhov [1966, p. 26], Pykhov [1973, pp. 26–29], Popov [1975, p. 5], and Kochubeeva [1977, pp. 62–66]. The distribution of ethanol by type of inputs used for 1966 and 1968 was derived from the reported quantities of commodities used and average production rates.

In addition to the use of agricultural commodities for the production of ethanol, table 4.4 shows the quantities of barley used in the production of beer, estimated on the basis of input data given in Vinogradov [1968, p. 280] and Shakhtan [1969, p. 295].

Soviet drinkers consume extremely large quantities of agricultural raw materials in the form of alcoholic beverages. An approximate order of magnitude can be suggested by the following calculation made for the late 1970s (excluding grapes and fruits used in winemaking): use of agricultural inputs in production of ethanol for alcoholic beverages converted to grain equivalents, 5.4 million tons; barley used in beer production, 1.5 million tons; use of agricultural inputs in production of samogon (see chapter 5.3), 4.8 million tons; total of 11.7 million tons. According to official Soviet statistics the total consumption of grain products by the population in the late 1970s amounted to about 45 million tons per year.[2] Thus consumption of alcohol, even excluding wine, used up about one quarter of the grains available to the population. Needless to say, this is only a rough approximation. Similar calculations can be performed in terms of the sugar-equivalence of alcohol or the caloric content of alcohol with almost identical results.

4.3 *Use of Wood-Hydrolytic Ethanol in Production of Alcoholic Beverages*

Evidence available from different sources indicates that in the late 1950s and the early 1960s significant quantities of synthetic ethanol were used secretly in the production of Soviet vodka and wines. This unfortunate practice apparently had a disastrous effect on the health of the Soviet people and was sharply reduced or discontinued in 1964. To present a complete picture of this development we must review some historical facts.

In the late 1940s the demand for ethanol was increasing rapidly both as the result of the return to peacetime levels of consumption of alcoholic beverages and because of the rapid restoration and growth of the synthetic rubber industry, which uses larger quantities of ethanol. The poor performance of Soviet agriculture and destruction in the war of ethanol distillation plants in the Ukraine and Belorussia caused a much slower growth of food-based ethanol production [Borisovich 1980, pp. 61–63]. The government concentrated its efforts on the expansion of synthetics, sulfite, and hydrolytic ethanol, but even the relative success of the growth of these sectors did not alleviate ethanol shortages. While the performance of Soviet agriculture improved somewhat, the growing demand for processed foods placed a premium on grains and potatoes. Expansion of the use of molasses and, later, of sugar beets in the production of ethanol was a short-term measure which did not solve the problem. Correctly foreseeing continuous pressure on agriculture, the Soviet government concentrated on the development of chemical substitutes for agricultural commodities. Substitution of ethanol produced from petroleum, gas, and wood, all of which were available in abundance, for ethanol produced from agricultural commodities, which continued to be scarce, was particularly attractive.

The desire to reduce the use of agricultural commodities for the production of ethanol was not the only reason for the experimental use of hydrolytic ethanol for human consumption. Another problem with the utilization of food-based ethanol

Table 4.4. Use of agricultural inputs in production of food-based ethanol, thousand tons

	Potatoes	Grain	Molasses	Sugar beets	Sugar	Barley for beer
1955	1,232	2,254	739	0	0	462
1956	1,561	1,589	1,276	0	0	452
1957	n.a.	n.a.	n.a.	0	0	492
1958	n.a.	n.a.	n.a.	n.a.	0	498
1959	n.a.	n.a.	n.a.	n.a.	0	580
1960	696	1,360	1,690	251	0	625
1961	n.a.	1,072	n.a.	913	n.a.	667
1962	465	1,168	1,806	954	848	705
1963	690	1,004	1,576	502	407	702
1964	1,634	1,280	1,578	440	5	708
1965	2,599	704	2,178	899	87	792
1966	1,996	655	2,019	906	388	859
1967	1,937	879	2,034	866	368	903
1968	2,688	898	2,263	734	252	958
1969	2,405	987	2,397	527	202	993
1970	2,072	1,148	1,792	432	680	1,048
1971	1,782	1,635	2,098	502	140	1,103
1972	n.a.	n.a.	n.a.	n.a.	n.a.	1,173
1973	2,005	2,420	2,074	0	0	1,270
1974	n.a.	n.a.	n.a.	n.a.	n.a.	1,350
1975	2,120	3,030	2,038	0	681	1,428
1976	n.a.	n.a.	2,900	n.a.	n.a.	1,480
1977	n.a.	n.a.	3,196	n.a.	n.a.	1,548
1978	n.a.	n.a.	n.a.	n.a.	n.a.	1,603
1979	n.a.	n.a.	n.a.	n.a.	n.a.	1,583

n.a.: Data are not available

was the seasonal deliveries which were determined by the harvest times of agricultural commodities. The demand for alcoholic beverages is fairly constant over the year [Druzhinin 1963, pp. 109–111] while the production of food-based ethanol is subject to seasonal fluctuations. In the early and mid-1950s, 72 percent of all ethanol was produced in the first and the fourth quarters of the year [Zotov 1958, pp. 188–189]. This pattern created problems with storage both of the commodities used for production and of the final product. Agricultural commodities, particularly potatoes and sugar beets, lose some of their nutrient value in prolonged storage, reducing the efficiency of production. The problems of storage of the finished product were also serious—ranging from inadequate storage facilities [Pykhov 1969, p. 28] to losses of stored ethanol due to evaporation.

Thus, from the point of view of managers and planners, the ideal arrangement would be to direct some food-based ethanol to be used for technical purposes in the periods when the supply exceeded the demand of the beverage industry and, conversely, to use some synthetic ethanol for human consumption during the

Table 4.5. Estimation of quantity of hydrolytic ethanol used in production of alcoholic beverages, millions of liters

	1	2	3	4	5	6		7		8	9	10		11
	Production of food ethanol (raw alcohol)	Food ethanol used for technical purposes (raw alcohol)	Left for human use	Imports	Total supply of raw ethanol	Supply of rectified ethanol for human use		Purified ethanol used in alcoholic beverages		Demand for ethanol in final products	Demand for ethanol for production	Difference between demand and supply		Average
						Low	High	Low	High					
1956	1,032	410	622	71	693	634	651	539	579	554	576	− 37	+ 3	− 17
1957	1,245	510	735	31	766	701	720	596	641	631	655	− 59	− 14	− 37
1958	1,160	457	703	30	733	671	689	570	613	663	689	− 119	− 76	− 98
1961	1,170	460	710	0	710	650	667	566	594	700	727	− 161	− 133	− 147
1962	1,323	458	865	66	931	852	875	741	779	789	820	− 79	− 41	− 60
1963	1,162	240	922	24	946	866	889	753	791	841	886	− 133	− 95	− 114
1964	1,112	48	1,064	61	1,125	1,030	1,058	896	942	884	919	− 23	+ 23	0

Column 1: From Table 4.1

Column 2: Aref'ev 1958, p. 27 and Pykhov 1966, p. 20.

Column 3: Column 1 minus Column 2.

Column 4: Standard Soviet foreign trade sources. Since all or most ethanol was imported from Cuba, we can assume that it was food-based.

Column 5: Column 3 plus Column 4.

Column 6: In the process of rectification of raw alcohol into purified alcohol a certain quantity of alcohol is lost because of removal of impurities and from other causes. Khalaim [1972, pp. 128–129] reports that the output of pure alcohol varies from 92.5 to 95 percent of raw alcohol used. In addition about 1 percent of alcohol is lost in storage and shipment [Pykhov 1973, pp. 250–253, and Kochubeeva and Shteiner 1974, p. 64]. We will use the range of 91.5 to 94% for the low and high estimates of pure ethanol obtained in purification.

Column 7: According to Pykhov [1966, p. 30] between 88 and 91 percent of food-based ethanol supplied is used in the production of vodka and in wine-making. The figures are clearly rough and possibly understated. Thus, in the second edition of his book, Pykhov [1973, p. 33] gives 90 to 98 percent. If, in fact, these two sets of ranges indicate a trend towards higher relative consumption of ethanol in production of alcoholic beverages the ratios for the late 1950s should be lower. Accordingly we will use a range of 85 to 89 percent for 1956–1958 and a range of 87 to 90 percent for the 1961–1964 period. These ratios are then applied to the low-high estimates given in Column 6.

Column 8: Demand for ethanol used in the production of vodka and vodka-based beverages, and in the fortification of wines is estimated on the basis of the data in Tables 1.1 and 2.5.

Column 9: In the process of mixing ethanol with water or wine, the volume of liquids is reduced and some heat is generated reducing the amount of alcohol in the final product. Thus, production of 1 liter of 40% vodka requires .416 liters of 100% ethanol. The figures in Column 8 were accordingly adjusted to reflect this loss [Mel'man et al., 1966, p. 131].

Column 10: The difference between the demand for ethanol for production of alcoholic beverages (Column 9) and the low-high estimates of supply (Column 7). Shortages shown with a minus sign suggest that synthetic alcohol was used.

Column 11: Averages of figures in Column 10.

months when the supply of food-based ethanol was insufficient. It is impossible to say when the Government made the decision, but the estimates made below suggest that the use of hydrolytic ethanol in the production of alcoholic beverages on a large scale started in 1956–1957.

It is not surprising that the introduction of hydrolytic alcohol for human consumption was effected during Khrushchev's leadership. Khrushchev was keenly aware of the deficiencies of Soviet agriculture, concerned with the insufficient supply of basic agricultural commodities to the population and, at the same time, considered the rapid development of the Soviet chemical industry a panacea for the problems besetting the Soviet economy. The hasty start of the dangerous experiment with hydrolytic alcohol is also in keeping with Khrushchev's character and his "harebrained schemes." In fact, it was Khrushchev himself who broke the secrecy surrounding the use of hydrolytic alcohol for human consumption in June 1961 at the Vienna meeting, when he "was boasting to Kennedy about Soviet feats, including a newly developed process of making vodka out of natural gas . . . ."[3] [Bradlee 1975, p. 125].

Table 4.5 shows the estimation of the level of hydrolytic alcohol used in the production of alcoholic beverages in the 1956–1964 period. The estimates are made on the basis of calculated demand for ethanol for vodka production, wine fortification, and for supply of food-based alcohol; they are explained in notes following the table. Because of the absence of key data, estimation was impossible for 1959 and 1960. Precise estimation is difficult and the true values lie probably somewhere in the range shown in Column 10. It will be noted that the quantities of hydrolytic ethanol used in the estimated production of alcoholic beverages are consistent with the quantities of hydrolytic ethanol produced.

Interesting supporting evidence for the estimated use of hydrolytic ethanol in the production of alcoholic beverages is found in Soviet input-output tables. The 1959 table showed the "forest chemistry and wood hydrolysis" sector selling 42.7 million rubles of products to the "processed food" sector producing, among other things, all alcoholic beverages [Ts.S.U. 1960, p. 143]. The 1966 table recorded the same transaction, but at a substantially reduced level of 4.3 million rubles [Ts.S.U. 1967, p. 109]. The data offered in input-output tables is in monetary terms, and the exact nature of products being sold is not given. However, knowing the commodity composition of the "wood hydrolysis" sector [Treml et al., 1972, p. 115], it is clear that only hydrolytic alcohol could have been purchased by the food industry at such levels. At 0.51 rubles per liter of wood-hydrolytic alcohol [Ryzhkov 1961, p. 225] the sale of 42.7 million rubles translates into a delivery of some 84 million liters, which is broadly consistent with the estimates made above.

The end of large-scale use of hydrolytic alcohol in the production of alcoholic beverages probably came in 1963. Pykhov, the leading authority on the Soviet alcohol industry, carefully notes that: "The question of the possible use of synthetic alcohol for human consumption was raised in 1958–1960. However, as the result of lengthy research the State Sanitary Inspector of the Ministry of Health of the

USSR ruled that synthetic alcohol cannot be used for food purposes." [Pykhov 1973, p. 33]

It is difficult to say, however, whether the use of hydrolytic ethanol for human consumption was completely banned in 1964 or was continued at a reduced level. The estimates made above suggest that by 1964 the supply of food-based ethanol was equal to demand, and thus the need for hydrolytic ethanol for production of beverages was reduced. Still, the seasonal fluctuations in the production of raw-food-based ethanol and the possible disruptions in the distribution system, which are so frequent in the USSR, could conceivably have required the periodic use of hydrolytic ethanol.

The use of wood-hydrolytic ethanol in production of alcoholic beverages could not be concealed from the population for too long. A high official of the Ministry of Food, who recently emigrated to the West, confirmed the use of synthetic alcohol "in large quantities in the production of vodka." According to this source, a plant producing vodka from synthetic alcohol was located on Sakhalin Island and was closed down upon Khrushchev's death [T1P 11–78 FF]. Synthetic vodka was termed "Suchek" or "wood knot" in popular slang [T2T 0–75 GG, T2T 8–81 DD, G4K 0–81 IM92] and this term found its way into literature [Mitin 1965, p. 13; Krasikov 1977, p. 113; *Vremia i my*, No. 17, 1977, p. 124]. The famous Russian balladeer and writer of underground songs, Vysotskii, mentioned "vodka made out of sawdust" in one of his songs composed in the 1960s [*Pesni* 1977, p. 49].

In the "Second Economy" émigré survey project, 93 émigrés out of 533 interviewed, reported having heard of the use of synthetic ethanol in the production of vodka. Most of the interviewees said that they had heard of this practice for the first time in the mid-1960s and continued to hear about it through the late-1970s. One émigré reported that his friend employed at the Dnistr vodka factory in Lvov told him that the use of synthetic ethanol in vodka was a common practice and the émigré himself saw large containers with synthetic alcohol [T2M 4–81 AM4]. Another émigré reported having heard about this practice from vodka factory workers [G4K 0–81 MT39]. This evidence suggests that the use of hydrolytic alcohol in the production of beverages was not terminated in 1963 but continued although probably at reduced levels.

This practice is of great importance in yet another facet of alcohol consumption in the USSR. The use of malodorous molasses, sugar beet, and wood hydrolytic ethanol in the production of vodka, and the general public knowledge of this, played an important role in encouraging the production and consumption of home-distilled illegal beverages, particularly samogon (see chapter 5). The poor taste and unpleasant odor of samogon have traditionally inhibited its use. It is not unreasonable to speculate that the deterioration of the quality of state-produced vodka, and particularly the use of hydrolytic ethanol, made samogon a more attractive substitute.

Most aspects of this experiment with the marketing of wood-hydrolytic ethanol for human consumption remain shrouded in secrecy. The actual chemical composition of the hydrolytic ethanol produced in this period is not known, and therefore its potential health hazards cannot be evaluated.

The termination of the large-scale use of hydrolytic ethanol in the production of alcoholic beverages came at a most unfortunate time for Khrushchev's government. As a result of the very poor 1963 harvest, the Soviet Union was forced for the first time in the post-war period to import several million tons of grain from western markets.[4] The decision to abandon the prospect of a gradual substitution of synthetic for food-based ethanol and to direct large quantities of grain and other produce back to the alcohol industry in 1963–1964 could not have been made lightly. This suggests indirectly that the potential ill effects of wood-hydrolytic ethanol must have been quite serious. In the absence of any additional information the task of an overall evaluation of the results of this experiment must remain open.

5. Production of Samogon and other Homemade Beverages

5.1 *Home-Distilled Samogon*

No study of production and consumption of alcoholic beverages in the USSR would be complete without a inquiry into the illegal home distillation which has traditionally contributed a major share of the total alcohol consumed in the country.

The wide-spread production of samogon[1] is explained by a variety of factors, such as the relatively high price of state-produced alcoholic beverages, the simplicity of the distillation process, which requires little specialized equipment, and the general availability of the main ingredients for production such as yeast, flour or grain, potatoes, sugar beets, or sugar. Sugar is a particular favorite of home brewers because it is both relatively less costly in terms of the final product and significantly less bulky than other possible raw materials such as potatoes or sugar beets.

Because of the primitive nature of home brewing, the final product, samogon, has more impurities than the standard ethanol-based vodka. Higher levels of fusel oils and of complex alcohols contribute to the strong and unpleasant odor and taste of samogon [Orlovskii 1975, p. 4; Livshits and Iavorskii 1975, pp. 21–22]. However, the pressures of shortages of agricultural inputs for the state ethanol industry led to the use of low-grade malodorous ethanol distilled from molasses and sugar beets. The use of poorly rectified ethanol for the production of the standard 40 percent vodka in the 1950s and 1960s, as well as the use of large quantities of hydrolytic ethanol (chapter 4), resulted in a significant lowering of the quality of most of the alcoholic beverages produced in the USSR. The quality gap between samogon and state-produced beverages was thus narrowed, making samogon a better substitute and contributing to its wider use.

Depending on the length of the distillation cycle and the skills of the producer, the alcohol content of samogon varies from 25 to 75 percent. One can reasonably expect that most of the samogon has about 40 percent alcohol, matching the alcohol content of standard Soviet vodkas. However, references in the literature and émigré interviews indicate that stronger varieties are also produced [*Krokodil*, No. 5, 1961, p. 3, No. 6, 1961, p. 4, No. 33, 1961, pp. 8–9, No. 8, 1974, p. 14, No. 34, 1975, p. 8; T3T 2–81MM; G1G 10–80AB; T3T 5–80UU]. It should be pointed out the mixture of ethanol and water can be ignited when the share of ethanol reaches 50 percent (the definition of 100 proof mixture). This feature offers a convenient test of the alcohol content of samogon—if a piece of cloth or of paper dipped into the brew can be ignited it means that the alcohol content is at least 50 percent. It is thus possible that 50 percent samogon is in higher demand in shady samogon markets as suspicious buyers can easily test the product.

Another factor to consider is the prohibition of production and marketing of state manufactured vodka of 50 and 56 percent alcohol content introduced during the anti-alcohol campaign of 1972. Drinkers with a preference for strong beverages were then likely to turn to the samogon markets.

The continuous attempts of the authorities to eradicate home distillation had little success because of the ubiquitous nature of the problem. In the United States, moonshine operations are usually undertaken by a dozen or so individuals working relatively large stills, which produce for a market. In contrast, in the USSR, production of samogon is done on a small scale by a large number of households and with only a fraction of samogon earmarked for sale outside the household. This, of course, makes the policing of illegal home brewing almost impossible.

The tentative nature of the estimates of samogon production made in this study cannot be overstressed. Soviet official statistical sources have not published any summary statistics on samogon production since the early 1930s. Policing as well as estimating the output of samogon is extremely difficult given the fact that a large and varying share of the rural population and, in all probability, a significant share of urban residents, are engaged in home distillation. In the 1920s the Central Statistical Administration made a study of samogon production on the basis of reports of special statistical correspondents located in practically all villages and rural settlements [Cherliunchakevich 1929]. It is doubtful that such a method could be tried at the present time or that it would produce accurate results because of much stiffer penalties for illegal home distillation. Thus, in all probability, Soviet authorities themselves do not have accurate year-by-year estimates of samogon production.[2]

The estimates made in this study, handicapped by an almost complete absence of summary statistical data, must be considered as first approximations with a significant probable error.

5.2 *Estimating Production and Consumption of Samogon*

In the absence of any external trade and any significant storage and changes in stocks, the production of samogon will be equated with its consumption. The basic assumption underlying estimating methods is that, subject to certain corrections, per capita consumption of pure alcohol in all forms in rural and urban areas is identical, and thus production of samogon on a per capita basis is estimated as the difference between per capita consumption of alcohol in the form of all state-produced beverages in urban and rural areas. The similarity of urban and rural levels of consumption is explained by the fact that urbanization of the USSR is a relatively recent phenomenon and that a majority of the urban population is the first or possibly the second generation of urban dwellers. Thus, social, family, and cultural ties between the rural and urban communities are still very strong.

The discussion of the accuracy of this method, the examination of some factors

Table 5.1. Annual expenditures on alcoholic beverages and consumption of absolute alcohol per capita by urban and rural areas (State-produced beverages only)

	Expenditures in rubles per capita*		Consumption in liters per capita*	
	Urban	Rural	Urban	Rural
1955	79.37	23.43	6.91	2.24
1956	78.78	24.13	6.89	2.31
1957	88.28	29.13	7.59	2.73
1958	93.65	33.03	7.01	2.64
1959	94.07	35.82	7.15	2.98
1960	101.31	38.89	7.68	3.22
1961	103.08	41.03	7.82	3.40
1962	112.60	42.64	8.47	3.47
1963	116.52	44.98	8.74	3.67
1964	132.06	49.04	8.80	3.92
1965	126.58	52.49	9.28	4.19
1966	135.33	58.10	10.13	4.56
1967	146.15	65.35	10.47	5.11
1968	154.85	68.95	11.19	5.45
1969	162.35	74.03	11.77	5.95
1970	169.32	82.46	11.69	6.32
1971	176.76	89.96	11.68	6.85
1972	181.40	97.29	11.95	7.20
1973	186.50	102.82	11.42	7.18
1974	192.25	108.47	11.35	7.57
1975	200.19	115.47	12.90	8.41
1976	204.60	120.83	13.28	8.94
1977	211.25	128.65	13.97	8.63
1978	215.24	135.28	12.73	8.72
1979	222.65	141.49	13.26	9.23

*Persons fifteen years and older.

likely to generate errors in the estimates, and a partial verification of the estimates based on some independent data will be found below.

The first task is to estimate consumption of pure alcohol per person fifteen years and older separately for urban and rural areas. This is done on the basis of available Soviet retail trade statistics. The state retail trade organizations serve mainly the urban population while the cooperative trade organizations are located in rural areas. Using the information provided in Fridman[1972, p. 14 and p. 82], Gladkaia [1974, p. 52] and Fridman [1976, p. 91], we can estimate the shares of cooperative trade sales in rural areas (see table 5.2).[3]

The first set of estimates of rural and urban per capita expenditures on alcoholic beverages is then calculated as follows:

Table 5.2. Supporting data used in samogon estimation

	Percentage of cooperative trade sales in rural areas	Expenditure on vodka as percent of total alcohol expenditure in rural areas	Samogon as percent of urban consumption of absolute alcohol
1955	73.4	90.0	5.0
1956	72.9	88.4	5.0
1957	72.4	86.9	5.0
1958	71.9	85.5	10.0
1959	71.2	84.0	10.0
1960	70.8	82.6	10.0
1961	70.3	81.3	10.0
1962	69.7	79.9	10.0
1963	69.2	78.6	10.0
1964	68.6	77.3	10.0
1965	68.1	76.0	10.0
1966	67.5	74.7	10.0
1967	66.9	73.4	10.0
1968	66.3	72.2	10.0
1969	65.7	71.0	10.0
1970	65.2	69.8	10.0
1971	64.8	68.7	10.0
1972	64.4	67.5	10.0
1973	64.0	66.4	11.0
1974	63.7	65.3	12.0
1975	63.2	64.2	13.0
1976	62.8	63.1	13.5
1977	62.4	62.1	14.0
1978	62.0	61.0	14.5
1979	61.6	60.0	15.0

a. Sales of "other foods" through cooperative trade organizations were obtained from standard Soviet statistical sources.
b. By applying correction factors referred to above, the sales of "other foods" through cooperative trade organizations were reduced to cover only the sales in rural areas.
c. The values of "other foods" sales in rural areas obtained in step *b* were reduced by 10 percent to remove miscellaneous foods leaving only alcoholic beverages (Section 3.2).
d. Sales of alcoholic beverages in rural areas obtained in step *c* were subtracted from total sales of alcoholic beverages estimated earlier (table 3.1), giving sales of alcoholic beverages in urban areas only.
e. Sales of alcoholic beverages in rural and urban areas were divided by population fifteen years and older in rural and urban areas giving expenditures on alcoholic beverages per capita.

The next task is to convert rural and urban per capita expenditures to per capita consumption of pure alcohol. This conversion rests on the crucial assumption concerning the differences in the mix of alcoholic beverages purchased in urban and rural areas. Rural incomes are substantially lower than urban incomes and we will thus expect the people in rural areas to buy more of the inexpensive vodka which offers the highest quantity of pure alcohol per ruble. Supply of alcoholic beverages to rural areas in the USSR has never been as diversified as in urban areas, and wines and beer were always less readily available.

It will be recalled that the share of vodka in total (urban and rural) expenditures declined from 71 percent in 1955 to 63 percent in 1965 and to 52 percent in 1979 (section 2.2). As a first approximation 90 percent is taken as the share of vodka in rural purchases of all alcoholic beverages in 1955, reducing it linearly to 60 percent in 1979. Making the reduction of the share of vodka in rural areas faster than in the country as a whole reflects the fact that rural incomes have been increasing faster than urban incomes and that the supply of alcoholic beverages in rural areas has been gradually improving. These estimates can be verified at least for one year—according to Lokshin [1975, p. 80],—vodka constituted 66 percent of total sales in cooperative stores in 1974 compared with our estimate of 65 percent.

It will also be assumed that the residual in the total expenditures on alcoholic beverages in rural areas is spent on wines, i.e., that no cognac, champagne, or beer is purchased. The exclusion of the first two is not unreasonable—the two beverages are costly in terms of the price of alcohol per ruble and, as a rule, are not associated with the rural way of life. The exclusion of beer is made for the sake of simplification and may generate a certain error. Beer is, of course, consumed in rural areas, but the quantities are small and difficult to estimate. In the mid-1960s Soviet specialists were noting that the "supply of beer to rural areas was poor" [Zotov et al., 1967, p. 417]. In the late 1960s a number of small breweries were built in rural areas, but by the mid-1970s consumption of beer by urban residents was 4 to 6 times higher on a per capita basis than consumption of beer by people living in villages [Elagina et al., 1975, pp. 24–28].

Based on these assumptions, the step-by-step calculations were made as follows:

f. Per capita ruble expenditures on alcoholic beverages estimated in step *e* above were multiplied by the percent share of vodka in rural expenditures, resulting in per capita expenditures on vodka.

g. Per capita expenditure on vodka was divided by the average price of vodka (table 3.2) and converted to pure alcohol by multiplication by average alcohol content of vodka (section 2.2). As the result, per capita rural consumption of pure alcohol is estimated in the form of vodka.

h. Per capita rural expenditures on wine were calculated by subtracting per capita expenditures on vodka (step *f* above) from per capita expenditure on all alcoholic beverages (step *e*).

i. Rural per capita consumption of pure alcohol in the form of wine was estimated as in step *g* above by dividing rural per capita expenditure on wine (step *h*) by the average price of wine and multiplying it times the average alcohol content of fruit, berry, and grape wines (section 2.2).

j. Adding together per capita consumption of pure alcohol in the form of vodka (step *g*) and wine (step *i*) gives rural per capita consumption of pure alcohol in all forms of beverages.

k. Per capita cosumption of pure alcohol in all forms of beverages in urban areas was then estimated on the basis of total consumption of alcohol by the entire population (table 2.5), per capita consumption in rural areas (step *j*), and the appropriate population statistics.

The estimates made in steps *j* and *k* are shown in table 5.1.

As was discussed above the method of estimating production and consumption of samogon in the USSR is based on the assumption that consumption of pure alcohol per person 15 years and older is identical in rural and urban areas. Thus, any difference in per capita consumption of state-produced alcoholic beverages is covered by samogon.

In an earlier study this author made the assumption that samogon production and consumption are primarily rural phenomena and that no significant quantities of samogon are produced or consumed in cities [Treml 1974, pp. 303–304]. However, the information which has become available since the earlier publication suggests that this assumption is not tenable and in fact urban dwellers have been consuming increasing quantities of samogon.[4] Soviet sources have been referring to samogon in urban areas more and more often and recent émigrés from the USSR reported a similar trend. Of the 494 émigrés who have answered the question in the "Second Economy" survey, 227 said that samogon is produced often in urban areas, 243 reported hearing of the practice infrequently, and only 24 said that they had never heard of production of samogon in urban areas.[5]

One of the primary causes for the emergence of samogon in the cities and its subsequent spreading is probably sugar. As will be discussed in greater detail below the relatively low price of sugar and the very rapid increase in Soviet production and consumption of sugar made samogon production much easier. In contrast to other possible inputs into samogon making such as grains, potatoes, or sugar beets, sugar was becoming generally available in cities in the late 1950s and early 1960s. Less bulky than other commodities and available at prices which were set in the mid-1950s, it was one of the cheapest commodities to be used.

Reflecting all this evidence, production and consumption of samogon will be estimated on the assumption that rural and urban per capita consumption of absolute alcohol are identical and that an increasing share of alcohol consumed in cities is in the form of samogon. Thus, the calculations will be done as follows:

Samogon 100 percent alcohol content $= (c_u \cdot s) \, P_u + [c_u \, (1 + r) - c_r] \, P_r$

where

   c   stands for consumption of state-produced alcoholic beverages converted to absolute alcohol per person fifteen years and older

P stands for population

s stands for percentage of urban per capita consumption of alcohol in the form of samogon

u (subscript) stands for urban

r (subscript) stands for rural

The estimation of samogon consumpton in urban areas was the most difficult and probably the least accurate part of the exercise. The following factors had to be considered:

— The upsurge of samogon making in 1958 caused by the 20 percent increase in prices of all state-produced alcoholic beverages.

— The gradual phasing out of inexpensive vodka from state stores in the mid and late 1960s.

— The introduction of the new 1960 Criminal Code of the RSFSR (followed by new codes in republics) and the 1962–1965 amendments reducing penalties for samogon making.

— Increased availability of sugar throughout the 1960s.

— Declared and disguised increases in prices of state-produced alcoholic beverages beginning in 1970 and continuing through the late 1970s.

— The imposition of restrictions on hours of sale of strong alcoholic beverages in state stores and other antidrinking measures of 1972, including revisions and reinterpretations of laws and regulations dealing with samogon making.

The estimates of samogon consumption in urban areas expressed in percent of consumption of state-produced alcoholic beverage per person fifteen years and older are shown in table 5.2. The estimates translate into consumption of less than one liter of samogon of 40 percent alcohol content per adult in 1955–1957, between two and three bottles per urban adult in the 1960s and about four bottles in the late 1970s.

Samogon drinking is probably concentrated among low income urban groups. Thus we can assume that there is a group of urban adults which drinks samogon almost exclusively, while the rest of the urban population drinks samogon only occasionally. If we were to assume that the urban population consists of a group which drinks only samogon and a group which drinks only state-produced beverages, the estimated ratios given above would mean that, for example, in 1975 14 million people (12 percent of the urban population) were exclusively samogon drinkers. Relaxing this condition, we will see that the estimates made here roughly correspond to Neznanskii's statement that 70–80 percent of the urban population drink state-produced beverages, and 20–30 percent drink samogon [Neznanskii 1979, p. 55].

The final set of estimates of consumption of samogon is shown in table 5.3. These estimates, derived by the method described above, were also checked against five independent sets of data as follows:

— Two prominent Soviet statisticians, Strumilin and Sonin, reported at a 1973 seminar that "at the present time consumption of samogon amounts to not less than 50 percent of vodka consumption," [Strumilin and Sonin 1974, p. 37].

- A recent Soviet émigré, and a former high official of the Ministry of Food of the USSR, reported in an interview that in the mid-1970s samogon production amounted to some 1,500–1,600 million liters [T3P 10–78 FF].
- A statement made by an authoritative Soviet statistician to this author indicated that "in the late 1970s samogon production exceeded 3 liters per capita" [T2T 0–0 II].
- Inferences which can be drawn from the excessive consumption of sugar which is the primary input into samogon production.
- Other selected quantitative data which can be used for the estimation of samogon production in the given year and locality such as those used in Treml [Treml 1975, pp. 307–308].

This method has obvious limitations. One is that we implicitly assume a population which is homogeneous with respect to rural-urban, sex, age, and ethnic proportions. Numerous Soviet studies as well as international experience suggest that women drink less than men. According to one Soviet study, adult females on the average consume about 25 percent of the amount of alcohol consumed by adult males, and the elderly of both sexes consume about 30 percent of the adult male consumption [Maier and Ershov 1971, p. 12]. Preferences for alcoholic beverages by type also differ by sex. Thus, women prefer wine to vodka and samogon is the least desirable beverage [Levin and Levin 1978, p. 12]. Lastly, Muslim ethnic groups consume significantly less alcohol than Slavs. Thus, as long as the urban and rural population of persons fifteen years and older are not identical in terms of the age, sex, and ethnic mix, the method used in this study will produce somewhat distorted results. However, the absence of the necessary data makes the adjustment for these factors impossible, although it is possible that some of the distortions would cancel each other out.

The second limitation of the method used is its mechanical nature, particularly the linear interpolation of the urban samogon consumption ratio. The estimates are, therefore, insensitive to factors which must have affected samogon consumption, such as changes in vodka prices, or poor harvests of sugar beets and potatoes. Again, the absence of the required statistics makes adjustment impossible. However, by and large, the estimates appear to be indicative of the correct order of magnitude and show realistic trends, and the use of the four sets of quantitative data listed above insures an acceptable level of accuracy.

5.3 Use of Agricultural Inputs in the Production of Samogon

Samogon can be distilled from a variety of products such as bread, flour, grains, potatoes, fruits, sugar beets, and sugar. Probably all of these products have been used in home distillation at one time or another during the period of this study, with the level of use determined by relative prices and supply of available products.

Table 5.3. Consumption of forty percent samogon in urban and rural areas, million liters

	Rural	Urban	Total
1955	956	57	1,013
1956	945	57	1,002
1957	1,000	66	1,066
1958	942	127	1,069
1959	892	134	1,026
1960	940	147	1,087
1961	923	154	1,077
1962	1,037	172	1,209
1963	1,056	181	1,237
1964	1,015	180	1,195
1965	1,066	206	1,272
1966	1,168	231	1,399
1967	1,127	249	1,376
1968	1,206	272	1,478
1969	1,232	295	1,527
1970	1,136	303	1,439
1971	1,031	314	1,345
1972	1,020	331	1,351
1973	935	360	1,295
1974	867	401	1,268
1975	1,032	512	1,544
1976	1,018	561	1,579
1977	1,203	630	1,833
1978	957	609	1,566
1979	977	668	1,645

One study based on the data collected in twelve regions of the USSR in the late 1950s or early 1960s indicated that 48.3 percent of samogon was made out of flour, 33.4 percent from sugar beets, 6.8 percent from sugar, and 11.5 percent from other unspecified products [Boldyrev et al. 1966, p. 22]. Unfortunately we do not have more information about this study and cannot, therefore, evaluate it. However, it appears that sugar plays a most important role in samogon making. Soviet sources and émigré reports strongly suggest that since the mid-1960s sugar has become the dominant input into samogon production throughout the USSR [Shumskii 1973, p. 6; Man'ko 1980, p. 4; Zhmyrev and Larionov 1971, p. 4; *Verkhovnyi sud* 1964, p. 13; Klianin 1980, p. 2; Matyshevskii, ed., 1980, pp. 79–92; G1G 10–80 AB, T2T 11–80 UU, T2T 8–80 OO, T2T 11–79 CC, T2T 11–79 BB, T3T 7–78 HH].[6]

Soviet authorities are, of course, aware of the use of sugar for illegal home production of samogon. In fact, speaking at the 21st Party Congress in 1959, Khrushchev announced the government's goal of expanding production of sugar in the USSR, and at the same time he referred to the dangers of home distillation and to the waste of sugar and other products in the production of samogon, demanding stricter laws against it [*Vneocherednoi* 1959, pp. 395–396]. In a recent book, a prominent Soviet specialist on consumption, Lokshin, discussed the excessive use of sugar by the population, linking it to the production of samogon [Lokshin 1975, pp. 117–121].

The reasons the samogon brewers prefer sugar are many. With sugar priced between 0.78 and 0.95 rubles per kg., and with the given rate of samogon distillation per kg. of input, sugar-based samogon is the cheapest to produce. Sugar is also one of the least bulky of all possible raw materials, which means that the home producers use smaller utensils and apparatuses, which are easier to conceal from the police. Since the expansion of domestic sugar refinery capacities and the growth of imports from Cuba, sugar has been generally readily available throughout the USSR in unrestricted quantities. And, lastly, some émigré reports suggest that sugar-based samogon is superior to samogon made from other inputs and, in fact, is better than some brands of state-produced vodka (GIG 10–80 AB).

The rate of production of samogon per kg. of sugar depends, of course, on the skill of the brewer and his equipment. Several major studies conducted by Soviet authorities in the 1920s indicated that, on the average, production of 1 liter of pure alcohol in the form of samogon requires between 2.3 and 3.1 kg. of sugar, or about 1.1 kg. per 1 liter of 40 percent samogon [Voronov 1926, p. 62 and Cherliunchakevich, ed., 1929, p. 39]. We can assume that home distillation remained fairly primitive[7] and that the rate of production did not change significantly. This is confirmed by émigré interviews cited above, which report on the average a rate of about 1 to 1.1 kg. of sugar per liter of 40 percent samogon. We will use this rate in this study.

If sugar is the main product used in home distillation, at the rate of production of 1 liter per 1.1 kg. of sugar, the production of 1,000–1,600 million liters of samogon estimated in this study would require very large quantities of sugar. We should, therefore, analyze the available data on production and consumption of sugar in the USSR to ascertain whether there is any evidence of large quantities of sugar being diverted into the production of samogon and whether the available data can throw any light on regional distribution of samogon making and changes in production over time.

We will concentrate our attention on direct per capita consumption of sugar. It must be noted that there are two types of sugar consumption statistics—total and direct. The latter shows sugar consumed directly in the form of sugar, while total consumption covers both direct consumption and the use of sugar in such products as confections, fruit preserves, juices, and other processed foods. The Nutrition Institute of the Academy of Medical Sciences of the USSR determined the "scientific norm" of total sugar consumption at 36.5 kg. per capita [Komarov and Cherniavskii 1973, p. 113]. The actual total sugar consumption per capita rose from about 28 kg. in 1960 to 38.8 kg. in 1970 to 42.8 kg. in 1979, greatly exceeding the norm. Total consumption of sugar, however, cannot be broken down by urban and rural areas or by republics and we will, therefore, concentrate on direct consumption of sugar in the form of sugar.

Per capita consumption of sugar, both total and direct, depends on a multitude of factors such as the prices of sugar and other goods, the traditional eating patterns of the country, and income and age distribution of the population. There are, however, certain regularities—thus per capita consumption of sugar increases with the economic development of the country and the growth of per capita real income, but then reaches a certain plateau or saturation point. As a rule once a country has reached this plateau, the per capita consumption for any given year varies little with respect to income of households. Thus, in the U.S. total per capita consumption of sugar more than doubled between 1875 and 1925 and then remained stable at about 45 kg. between 1925 and the present. Direct consumption of sugar remained virtually constant at about 18 kg from 1947 through 1972.[8]

We will define the direct consumption of sugar in the USSR as consisting of sugar purchased by the population through retail trade plus sugar received by sugar beet growers in an incentive scheme. The latter should be explained in some detail as it provides an important channel for sugar into rural areas. The incentive scheme, which was introduced in 1956, provided for sales of sugar to sugar beet growers at reduced prices of 0.38 rubles per kg, compared with the state retail price of 0.78 rubles per kg in sugar producing regions. These sales were set at 5 kg of sugar per ton of sugar beets delivered by kolkhozes and at 2.5 kg for sovkhozes. Sugar sold at the low price to sugar beet growers could be either retained for their use or could be resold to the cooperative trade network at state retail prices. The latter arrangement, of course, simply amounted to an additional payment of 0.4 rubles per ton of beets delivered [Moreinis 1968, pp. 89–92; Buzulukov 1969, p. 294–295; and Lokshin 1975, pp. 119–121]. The data on the incentive sales for selected years are summarized in Table 5.4.

As can be seen from these statistics, the quantity of sugar sold under the incentive scheme to sugar beet growers was steadily increasing, while the reselling of this sugar to the state dropped to almost insignificant amounts after 1960. Thus the quantity of low-cost sugar retained in rural areas was continuously growing. It must be stressed that by the mid-1960s per capita consumption of sugar obtained from all sources in rural areas reached the level of urban consumption and continued to grow. The fact that sugar beet growers were retaining increasing quantities of sugar, despite the financial advantages offered by the opportunity to resell it, suggests that sugar was being used for other purposes than direct consumption of sugar.

The data on direct per capita consumption of sugar broken down into three general regions of the USSR are presented in table 5.5. The RSFSR[9] and a region combining the Ukraine and Belorussia are shown separately because, as regions with large concentrations of Slavic rural populations, they are most likely to be the areas of significant samogon production. Ideally, Moldavia should have also been included in this combined region, but the absence of published data on consumption of sugar made it impossible. The "rest of the USSR" region can be considered as the first approximation to represent the areas least likely to produce samogon in large quantities. They consist of the three Baltic republics, where average incomes

Table 5.4. Sales and disposition of sugar sold to sugar beet growers in selected years, thousand tons

Average	Sold to sugar beet growers at low prices	Resold by sugar beet growers to trade network at retail prices	Sugar retained by sugar beet growers
1956-1960	211	70	141
1961-1965	266	13	253
1966-1970	355	12	343
1971-1975	325	7	318

are sufficiently high to enable most drinkers to buy state-produced beverages, of the five Muslim republics where the consumption of alcoholic beverages, particularly vodka, is generally lower than in Slavic and Baltic areas, and of the two non-Muslim wine-producing Caucasian republics, Armenia and Georgia, where consumption of strong beverages is relatively low. Of course some production of samogon takes place in all of these republics, but probably at much lower levels on a per capita basis. The data in table 5.5 are estimated using published sales of sugar in value terms converted to kilograms on the basis of available prices.

An examination of the data for the two Slavic regions in table 5.5 shows that per capita consumption of sugar was lower in rural areas in the mid-1950s but that the gap was essentially closed by the mid- and late-1960s. Per capita consumption of sugar in rural areas continued to grow faster, with the result that by the early 1970s per capita consumption in rural areas exceeded that of urban areas. (Direct data on the rural-urban per capital consumption in the RSFSR are not available, but given the relative sizes of the population of the three regions and the per capita consumption in the USSR as a whole, it should be apparent that by the early 1970s rural per capita consumption in the RSFSR exceeded the urban level.)

Per capita consumption of sugar in the form of sugar appears to be excessive in the two Slavic regions, both compared with the rest of the country and in absolute terms. It would be very difficult to determine with any degree of accuracy what constitutes the saturation point in sugar consumption. In the USSR from the late 1960s to the present, a level of about 22 to 26 kg per capita seems to be reasonable. The data on the rest of the USSR supports this estimate. We can argue that since rural incomes in the USSR are much lower than urban incomes, the saturation point is achieved when rural and urban per capita consumption of sugar are at such levels that even the low income rural residents can afford to buy the same quantity of sugar as the more affluent city dwellers.[10]

The 22–26 kg estimate is also broadly confirmed by the fact that the "rest of the USSR" consumption of sugar per capita reached a plateau at this level in the late 1960s to the early 1970s. Another confirmation is found in the per capita consumption of sugar for a series of years, which can be estimated for the city of Moscow. In the 1955–1965 period the per capita consumption of sugar was about 28 kg with

Table 5.5. Per capita consumption of sugar in selected regions, kg per capita, all ages

	USSR			Ukraine-Belorussia			RSFSR			Rest of the USSR		
	Total	Urban	Rural	Total	Urban	Rural	Total	Urban	Rural	Total	Urban	Rural
1956	14.0	24.5	5.4	15.8	24.5	7.2	12.5	27.0	3.5	10.7	21.6	3.5
1957	15.3	26.2	5.9	16.7	26.0	7.2	14.6	31.2	4.5	11.9	22.2	4.5
1958	16.4	26.5	7.1	17.9	30.0	9.0	15.8	29.2	5.6	12.8	25.1	4.6
1959	17.4	27.2	8.3	18.7	27.1	9.3	18.0	32.9	6.2	13.1	20.0	8.4
1960	19.3	27.6	11.2	21.3	26.7	14.8	19.0	31.1	9.1	14.0	26.0	5.5
1961	20.6	27.3	13.8	22.6	27.4	16.7	20.4	29.6	12.4	15.4	24.2	9.0
1962	21.7	26.7	16.4	23.5	25.1	21.4	22.1	29.8	15.3	16.4	28.5	7.5
1963	23.4	28.0	18.4	25.3	26.5	23.6	24.0	31.1	17.5	17.7	29.2	9.4
1964	23.2	29.0	16.6	25.2	28.0	21.3	22.9	30.9	15.3	18.3	30.4	9.0
1965	23.9	27.9	19.4	25.3	26.2	23.9	25.5	32.5	18.8	18.9	28.1	11.6
1966	24.8	26.4	22.1	26.5	26.1	27.0	26.1	30.7	21.5	19.2	25.9	13.8
1967	26.2	27.4	24.6	27.8	26.4	30.0	28.5	31.2	25.7	19.8	26.4	14.1
1968	26.4	26.7	25.9	28.4			29.8	30.4	29.3	17.9		
1969	26.4	26.7	26.1	27.9			31.4	33.9	28.5	18.0		
1970	27.1	26.6	27.8	29.5			30.2	29.6	31.0	18.5		
1971	28.1	27.1	29.5	29.9			32.7	30.8	24.0	19.6		
1972	27.9	26.6	29.6	28.4			30.7	28.7	33.1	24.0		
1973	28.9	27.4	31.1	30.0			34.2	33.4	35.4	21.3		
1974	28.3	26.6	31.0	29.9			32.2	29.3	36.1	21.2		
1975	29.1	27.3	32.0	30.7			33.3	31.4	36.0	21.7		
1976	29.6	27.1	33.2	29.9			34.4	31.2	38.9	24.3		
1977	29.5	27.5	32.8	29.8			34.3	32.6	38.7	23.9		
1978	29.2	27.1	32.9	30.6			33.4	30.0	38.6	22.6		

very little variability, dropping to an almost constant 26 kg in the 1970–1979 period. It would be reasonable to assume that per capita incomes in Moscow are higher than average USSR incomes and that, therefore, the plateau reached at about 26 kg represents a saturation point.[11]

The 22–26 kg range as the likely saturation point can be verified in yet another way. As was pointed out above, the "scientific" norm of total per capita consumption of sugar has been estimated by Soviet authorities at 36.5 kg. In the early 1970s the ratio of the actual total per capita consumption to direct per capita consumption of sugar has been about 1.45. Applying this ratio to the "scientific" norm, we can calculate the norm for direct per capita consumption at about 25 kg or within the ranges suggested above. Presumably, the "scientific" norm does not include sugar to be used for production of samogon and thus should be more or less at the same level as the saturation point.

The estimated 22–26 kg as the range for the average per capita consumption of sugar in the form of sugar fully supports the estimates of samogon production made in Section 5.2.

At the rate of 1.1 kg of sugar per liter of 40 percent samogon, the excess sugar (i.e., actual per capita consumption less the consumption of sugar as sugar) consumed in the 1970s would be sufficient to produce anywhere from 1,000 to 1,700 million liters of samogon. In fact, rough calculations suggest that the excess sugar consumption estimated in this manner, broken down either by rural-urban areas or by regions of the USSR, corresponds approximately to separate estimation of samogon production broken down the same way.

5.4 Production of Samogon: Prices and Costs

The price of samogon is determined by a variety of factors such as alcohol content, prices of commodities used in its production, prices of vodka and other state-produced beverages, prices of bottles and glassware, and the risk involved in home distillation.

A sample of about 50 prices of samogon covering the period between the mid-1960s and the late 1970s was collected for the purposes of this study [Radio Liberty files; Zhmyrev and Larionov 1971, p. 4; Rutman 1979, p. 75; Neznanskii 1979, p. 54; Matyshevskii, ed., 1980, pp. 95–96; *Krokodil* No. 7, 1961, p. 4; T3P 11–78 FF, T3T 7–78 HH; G4K 0–76 KS; T2A 2–81 AC; T2A 3–81 AB; T3T 2–81 MM; and the special émigré questionnaire in which 37 families out of 358 reported having purchased samogon]. These price data are still difficult to evaluate because the quality and the alcohol content of samogon are usually not known. Thus, the results must be interpreted with caution. It appears that samogon is usually less expensive in remote rural areas than in larger settlements or in cities. Prices reflect the quality of samogon, usually in terms of commodities used for its preparation: drinkers consider samogon made out of sugar to be the best, followed by grain, flour, and sugar beets. Samogon made out of potatoes is considered to be the poorest and may cost 25 to 50 percent below the price of sugar-based samogon [*Krokodil* No. 8, 1964, p. 8; T2A 2–81 AC; G1G 11–80 AB].

In 1927 about 56 percent of all the samogon produced in rural areas was for home use [Cherliunchakevich 1929, p. 37]. According to a sample survey of some 12 regions made in 1958, about 95 percent of the samogon was produced for home use [Boldyrev et al. 1966, p. 22], but this ratio appears to be too high. For instance, in 15 cases of arrested samogon makers reported in a 1980 source, the average quantity of samogon and mash confiscated per household was about 160 liters— quantities which suggest production for outside markets [Matyshevskii, ed., 1980, pp. 79–95]. There is other evidence of significant quantities of samogon produced for commercial purposes [G1G 11–80 AB]. It is, of course, also possible that the share of samogon produced for commercial purposes has increased since 1958.

It must be stressed that even production for commercial purposes in the USSR is relatively small scale.[12] While there are some reports of stills located in remote areas, all the available evidence suggests that samogon is produced in small batches and, as a rule, in a kitchen or a barn by members of a household. Slightly more than half of those engaged in home brewing of samogon are women [Matyshevskii, ed., 1980, pp. 79–95; Boldyrev et al. 1966, p. 22].

Samogon prices were fluctuating between 2.5 and 4 rubles per liter in the early and mid-1960s, averaging about 4 rubles in the early 1970s and rising to 4.5 to 5 rubles by the mid- and late 1970s. Thus the price of samogon is usually about one-half of the price of state-produced vodka. This relationship seems to hold over time: for example, in 1924 samogon with an alcohol content of 40 percent was priced at 0.7 (old) rubles per liter compared with the price of state vodka of 1.57 [Cherliunchakevich ed., 1929, p. 42]. Chacha produced in the Caucasus is usually priced higher than samogon—the price rose from 5 rubles per liter in the early 1960s to 6 rubles in the late 1970s [*Verkhovnyi sud* 1964, p. 13; T3T 1–77 HH; T3T 10–80 PP].

It is important to estimate the share of samogon produced for home use and for commercial purposes, but it is virtually impossible to do so with any degree of accuracy. One problem is the grey area of samogon produced neither for consumption by household members nor for sale, but for various festive occasions or for hired outside help as primary or supplementary payment.

The cost of production of samogon can be estimated only approximately. As was indicated above, samogon is produced mainly from sugar, with an averge rate of production of about 1.1 kg of sugar per liter of 40 percent samogon. Depending on the region, the state price of sugar has ranged from 0.78 to 0.95 rubles per kg in state stores and 0.38 rubles per kg when purchased by sugar beet growers.

The only other major ingredient of samogon making is yeast, used at a rate of 50 grams per liter at a cost of 3.5 kopekas [G1G 10–80 AB]. The cost of fuel, other possible inputs, and depreciation on the equipment used, would add probably another 5–10 kopekas, and the cost of the bottle, based on the vodka-bottle deposit price, another 12 kopekas. Thus, the average cost of materials used in samogon-making ranges between 0.7 and 1.3 rubles per liter.

Labor inputs into production of samogon are also difficult to estimate with any degree of precision. According to a 1924 source, the output was not more than 23 liters of 40 percent samogon per work day [Chetyrkin 1924, p. 84]. Except for the universal use of sugar instead of grains, flour, or potatoes, the technology of home brewing has not changed appreciably since the 1920s. One could speculate that production of samogon from sugar, which is less bulky than other inputs, would make the process less labor intensive. On the other hand, the length of the work day has been reduced since the 1920s, thus cancelling the sugar factor. We can conclude that in all probability the labor output in home brewing remained at about the same level, i.e., 20–25 liters of 40 percent samogon per day. Using the average state wage of about 1 ruble per hour the labor input would add another 35–40 kopekas to the cost of producing one liter of samogon.

There are, of course, additional costs, such as the marketing of samogon and the risk of being apprehended, but by and large production of samogon appears to be highly profitable.

5.5 *Production of Homemade Wine, Beer and Braga*[13]

In addition to samogon, Soviet households, particularly in rural areas, produce a variety of other alcoholic beverages such as grape wine, fruit and berry wines, beer, and braga. As a rule the wines are produced by natural fermentation without fortification and have an alcohol content of between 10 and 12 percent. Beer and braga produced from grains (barley) and flour have 4–8 percent alcohol; there are also some reports that homemade braga is much more potent [*Vneocherednoi* 1959, pp. 240–24; *Krokodil* No. 15, 1959, p. 12 and No. 35, 1966, p. 15].

Production of these homemade beverages is legal provided they are consumed within the household and the products used in their preparation were not stolen. The law is somewhat confusing in this respect—the main test is the production process. Thus, beverages produced by distillation are illegal, while those produced by fermentation are legal for noncommercial purposes [Matyshevskii, ed., 1980, pp. 81–82]. The extent of prohibition of commercial production is also unclear. For instance, a statistical handbook for the Lithuanian republic reported sales of homemade wine in urban farmers' markets in the late 1960s and early 1970s. Some homemade wines were reportedly sold in farmers' markets in Moldavia [*Sovetskaia Moldavia*, June 22, 1972, p. 4].

The large-scale production of homemade wine is possible because a large share of grapes, fruits, and berries are grown in private plots and in private gardens. Our estimates of output of homemade grape wine are based on the estimated private production of grapes. Soviet statistical sources regularly publish data on gross output of grapes by the state sector (kolkhozes and sovkhozes) and by private growers, and on state procurement of grapes from all producers. Thus, as the first step in the estimation procedure, the quantity of grapes retained by private growers after state deliveries was calculated on the basis of published statistics.[14]

No information on the final disposition of grapes by private growers is available, but it appears that a large share is used for wine making. Grapes are perishable and difficult to transport without adequate refrigeration and packaging, and we can thus assume that private growers produce little or no table grapes for marketing in urban farmers' markets. In the state sector, about 90 percent of all grapes purchased by the state procurement agencies are earmarked for the wine industry with the rest sold fresh or used in the production of juices. We will use the same 90–10 division for privately grown grapes.

As the last step in the estimating procedure, we will convert the 90 percent of grapes retained by private growers into wine, on the basis of a constant ratio of 665 liters of wine of 11 percent alcohol content per ton of grapes [Zaiats et al., 1969, p. 330]. The estimates are shown in table 5.6.

As can be seen from the tabulated data, the output of homemade wine estimated here is small relative to the state-produced wines. On a per capita basis its importance is also rather small. It rose from some 0.2 liters of absolute alcohol in the late 1950s to about 0.35 liters in the late 1960s and 1970s per person fifteen years and older.

It should be noted, however, that the production of homemade wine is highly differentiated by region. Thus, on a regional basis, production and per capita consumption of homemade wine can be quite important. Using the same procedure as outlined above, we have estimated the production of homemade wine by republics in table 5.7. The estimates are for 1967, since this is the year for which regional per capita consumption of alcohol has been estimated in this study (see chapter 6).

Presumably all or most of the homemade grape wine is consumed within households, but, as was pointed out above, some homemade wine does make its way into urban farmers' markets. No data on prices of homemade grape wine were found in the literature. However, it is reasonable to assume that the price, were the wine sold, would be in the neighborhood of the prices of ordinary grape and fruit wines produced by kolkhozes and sold through cooperative trade outlets in rural areas and in small towns. These prices, easily calculable from published retail trade statistics, remained fairly stable at about 1.10–1.30 rubles per liter from the mid-1950s through the mid-1960s. Between 1966 and 1975, the average price of these wines rose from 1.20 to 1.90 rubles per liter.

The cost of producing homemade grape wine is determined by the cost of grapes. In the 1960s and 1970s state procurement prices for grapes ranged from 250 to 480 rubles per ton [Lastivkin, ed., 1973, pp. 168–170]. Thus the cost of grapes would fall in the range between 0.4 and 0.7 rubles per liter of wine, to which we should probably add 0.1–0.2 rubles to account for labor and fuel.

It is virtually impossible to estimate production of homemade fruit and berry wines with any degree of accuracy and we can just speculate about the probable order of magnitude. In the 1970s more than 5 million tons of fruits and berries were harvested annually on private plots and in private gardens in the USSR. However, unlike grapes, most fruits and berries are easy to transport and market, and with the strong demand in urban areas, a large share of total private production is probably sold. Using some approximations we can estimate that in 1967 (the last year

Table 5.6. Production of homemade grape wine, millions of liters

1955	183	1964	335	1973	622
1956	190	1965	452	1974	530
1957	218	1966	383	1975	641
1958	270	1967	468	1976	619
1959	251	1968	530	1977	497
1960	271	1969	495	1978	539
1961	374	1970	518	1979	599
1962	445	1971	552		
1963	385	1972	455		

Table 5.7. Production and consumption of homemade grape wine by republic, 1967

	Production of wine mill. liters	Consumption of wine per capita,* liters of absolute alcohol
USSR	468	0.312
RSFSR	32	0.038
Ukraine	81	0.258
Uzbekistan	44	0.808
Kazakhstan	5	0.071
Georgia	82	2.814
Azerbaidzhan	11	.450
Moldavia	120	6.053
Tadzhikistan	6	.465
Armenia	11	.883
Turkmenistan	4	.406

*Per person 15 years old and older.

for which the data are available), about 44 percent of total private production of fruits and berries was sold in urban markets. An unknown but probably significant share is also consumed fresh in rural areas.

Nevertheless, with one kg of fruits yielding between 1 and 3 liters of homemade wine of 10 percent alcohol content,[15] private growers should have enough fruits and berries left after marketing and home consumption to produce large quantities of wine. The rapid growth in consumption of state-produced fruit and berry wines (chapter 1) testifies to their growing popularity, and it seems that we are justified in assuming that private growers would use a part of their output for winemaking.

In the late 1970s, state-produced fruit and berry wines were selling at about 1.50 rubles per liter, while the cost per liter to private producers, depending on the fruits used and the yield of wine per kg, would range from 0.40 to 1.00 rubles per liter. Thus, while not as financially rewarding as samogon distillation or grape wine making, the production of homemade fruit wine is still attractive. We cannot extend this analysis any further without much additional research. But in light of this evidence we can speculate that in the late 1970s production of homemade fruit and berry wines could fall anywhere between 0.5 and 1.5 billion liters, thus adding between 0.25 and 0.75 liters of absolute alcohol to the per capita consumption in the USSR.

As is the case with grape wines, the production of fruit and berry wines is highly differentiated by regions and republics in the USSR. While no accurate estimation is possible, we can approximately rank the republics by probable per capita consumption on the basis of production statistics. Thus, we can calculate the quantities of fruits and berries grown by private growers, adjusted for state procurement, to determine the potential productive base for home wine making. Secondly, we can approximately determine demand for fruit and berry wine by republic by looking at state production of these wines, for it should roughly correspond to local tastes and preferences. Using these data we can conclude that per capita production of homemade fruit and berry wines in the late 1960s and 1970s in the Ukraine, Belorussia, Georgia and the three Baltic republics was three to four times higher than the national average.

A large variety of other alcoholic beverages such as fermented honey, beer, braga, and kvas is produced privately, but unfortunately it is virtually impossible even to guess at the quantities involved. All we have is some scattered evidence such as an émigré report of widespread private production of beer in the Baltic republics [G1G 10–80 AB], émigré reports of strong braga in Moscow and in rural areas [T2T 8–81 AD, T2T 10–81VV], and references to home production of beer and braga in the literature [*Novyi mir*, No. 12, 1962, p. 25; *Krokodil*, No. 15, 1959, p. 12, and No. 35, 1966, p. 15; Amalrik 1970, pp. 174–175; Tkachevskii 1974, p. 125; *Sovetskaia Kirgiziia*, September 29, 1972, p. 4; *Nash sovremennik*, No. 8, 1981, p. 25]. A knowledgable émigré, a former Moscow attorney, reported the widespread practice of making strong braga in Moscow bakeries in the early 1970s. The braga was produced for managers and visiting dignitaries but apparently not for sale [T2T 10–81 SS].

High taxes on state produced beer (see chapter 3) make home production from inexpensive inputs financially attractive. However, the main reason for widespread home brewing of beer and braga lies with periodic shortages of beer and kvas in the state distribution system, particularly in rural areas [Zotov et al., eds., 1967, p. 417; *Krokodil* No. 2, 1966, p. 4, No. 26, 1977, p. 11, No. 16, 1978, p. 13; *Sovetskaia Rossiia*, June 3, 1981, p. 2 and June 5, 1981, p. 4]. Faced with these shortages the peasants turn to their long-lived skills of home brewing. The quantities of beer and braga produced are probably significant,[16] but no estimation is possible.

As was estimated above, in the 1970s homemade grape wine added about 0.35 liters to consumption of absolute alcohol per person fifteen years and older. Production of homemade fruit and berry wines, estimated with a wide margin of probable error, could add anywhere from 0.25 to 0.75 liters to per capita consumption. Since estimation of production of homemade beer and braga is impossible, it would be prudent to conclude this section by suggesting that, in all probability, homemade production of alcoholic beverages other than samogon added in the 1970s about one liter to the consumption of absolute alcohol per person fifteen years and older.

6. Per Capita Consumption of Alcohol in the USSR

6.1. Average Per Capita Consumption

Per capita consumption of state-produced alcoholic beverages and of samogon, converted to absolute alcohol based on estimates made earlier (tables 2.5 and 5.3), is shown in table 6.1. It should be noted that the data in Table 6.1 do not include other homemade beverages such as grape, fruit and berry wine, beer, and braga. As was discussed in Section 5.5, the consumption of homemade wine was about 0.2 liters of absolute alcohol in the 1950s and the early 1960s and rose to 0.35 liters in the 1970s per person fifteen years and older. It proved impossible to estimate the production of homemade fruit and berry wines, beer, and braga, particularly in the earlier years. In the late 1970s a conservative estimate of consumption of all legally made home beverages is about one liter of absolute alcohol per person.

Another important source of alcohol for consumption, not included in statistics in this study, is the large scale theft of various types of ethanol from industrial enterprises, trade organizations and stores, and in transit. Theft of alcohol from railroads is frequently reported in Soviet media, and the quantities are often high—according to one report, about 7 million liters of pure alcohol were stolen from railroads of the RSFSR in 1972 [Babushkin 1974, p. 27]. Theft of alcohol from places of employment is also significant.[1] In the émigré survey, 81 out of 533 families or single individuals interviewed reported having regularly taken alcohol from their places of employment. The quantities taken varied from 1 to 180 liters of pure alcohol per year, averaging about 16.1 liters per year per respondent. A special study of the theft of alcohol in the USSR is required, but it appears that theft would add approximately 1 liter of absolute alcohol to the per capita data summarized in Table 6.1. Some of the stolen alcohol is probably synthetic or denatured and of poor quality with many impurities.

Per capita consumption of alcohol, averaged for the entire country (table 6.1), can be misleading or inaccurate as a measure of change in drinking patterns if we are dealing with a heterogeneous population. International experience tells us that per capita consumption of alcohol differs significantly by age, sex, and ethnicity of drinkers, among other factors. Thus, some inquiry into the age, sex and ethnic structure of the Soviet population is required to fully assess the per capita data shown here.

Unfortunately, almost no information on the distribution of Soviet drinkers by age, sex, and ethnicity is available beyond general and unquantifiable references such as "alcoholism is growing faster among women . . ." and "the age at which minors are introduced to drinking is lower now . . ." [Levin and Levin 1978, p. 12;

Table 6.1. Consumption of pure alcohol per person 15 years and older

	State-produced beverages		Samogon	State and Illegal beverages*	
	All beverages	Strong beverages		All beverages	Strong beverages
1955	4.39	3.34	2.87	7.26	6.21
1956	4.45	3.46	2.78	7.23	6.24
1957	5.04	3.87	2.92	7.96	6.79
1958	4.79	3.65	2.91	7.70	6.56
1959	5.09	3.71	2.78	7.87	6.49
1960	5.52	3.90	2.93	8.45	6.83
1961	5.72	4.01	2.87	8.59	6.88
1962	6.14	4.28	3.18	9.32	7.46
1963	6.41	4.37	3.21	9.62	7.58
1964	6.60	4.46	3.05	9.65	7.51
1965	7.02	4.69	3.19	10.21	7.88
1966	7.70	4.87	3.45	11.15	8.32
1967	8.18	5.23	3.34	11.52	8.57
1968	8.78	5.54	3.53	12.31	9.07
1969	9.36	5.63	3.59	12.95	9.22
1970	9.54	5.35	3.33	12.87	8.68
1971	9.80	5.18	3.05	12.85	8.23
1972	10.13	5.18	3.02	13.15	8.20
1973	9.84	5.38	2.84	12.68	8.22
1974	10.51	5.30	2.73	13.24	8.03
1975	11.31	5.57	3.27	14.58	8.84
1976	11.78	5.55	3.29	15.07	8.84
1977	11.50	5.56	3.77	15.27	11.12
1978	11.40	5.72	3.18	14.58	8.90
1979	11.94	5.71	3.30	15.24	9.01

*Without homemade grape, fruit and berry wine, beer, and braga, which would add at least one liter of alcohol to per capita consumption in the 1970s, and without stolen industrial alcohol.

Kuznetsova 1976, p. 13; Gindikin 1979, p. 3; Vaksenberg 1975, p. 12]. Thus we have to use indirect evidence and inferences from partial data to make some assessment of the per capita data. According to one authoritative study prepared by the State Planning Committee of the USSR (Gosplan), a woman of working age or an elderly person of either sex consume, respectively, 25.7 and 30.4 percent of the alcohol consumed by a man of working age [Maier and Ershov 1971, p. 112]. Unfortunately, the authors do not indicate the period for which this relationship was observed, but references indicate that the data were collected in the early 1960s.

Since the drinking habits of elderly people are largely determined by their drinking at earlier ages, we can assume that the working age to male-female drinking ratio holds true in retirement. Based on this assumption, we can break the percentage given for the elderly of both sexes (30.4) into 68.6 percent for elderly men and 17.6 percent for elderly women.[2] Weighting these ratios by 1960 population statistics and using the total consumption of alcohol in that year (table 2.2) we can

Table 6.2. Age-sex specific consumption
of alcohol, liters of pure alcohol

Men of working age (15-59)	10.1
Women of working age (15-54)	2.6
Elderly men (60 and over)	6.9
Elderly women (55 and over)	1.8
average for all groups	5.5

calculate age-sex-specific per capita consumption of alcohol data as is shown in table 6.2 follows (excluding samogon).

Using these age-sex-specific per capita figures with the corresponding population statistics we can estimate consumption of alcoholic beverages in 1979 as 1,122 million liters. That is, were the age-sex-specific per capita consumption unchanged, the growth of the population and the change in the population structure would have resulted in total consumption of alcohol in 1979 of 1,122 million liters. Instead, the actual consumption was 2,378 million liters (table 2.5), suggesting that the increase in drinking in the 1960–1979 period was not caused by the age-sex changes in the structure of the population but by increases in per capita consumption.[3]

International comparisons of per capita consumption of alcohol are fraught with statistical and methodological difficulties but are, nevertheless, instructive. Comparison of the Soviet data summarized in Table 6.1 offers some interesting insights and places the USSR in a proper international perspective. One factor which makes comparison of Soviet alcohol consumption with other countries particularly difficult is the significant share of samogon in the total alcohol consumed. Legal and illegal home production of distilled spirits and of wine probably takes place in many countries but consistent estimates are not readily available.

In some countries such as France and West Germany, home production of limited quantities of spirits and wine is legal as long as it is for consumption within households. It also appears that home-produced alcohol is included in published per capita consumption. In other wine growing countries such as Italy, home-produced wine is not recorded [Sulkunen 1978, pp. 44–48]. A careful study of unrecorded consumption of alcohol in Finland covers not only home production of wine and distilled spirits but also the drinking of industrial alcohol, alcohol surrogates, and smuggled alcohol. According to this study the ratio of unrecorded to recorded consumption dropped below 10 percent in the 1970s [Makela 1979, pp. 62–71]. Consumption of moonshine in the US can be roughly estimated at about 2 percent of recorded consumption in 1977 but was probably higher in earlier years [Hyman et al. 1980, p. 10].

It appears that the legal home production of home spirits and wines is included in most international statistics while the difficult-to-obtain data on illegal production are not. However, the latter are probably a relatively small share of total consumption of alcohol and can thus be disregarded. On the other hand, samogon accounted for as much as 65 percent of total alcohol consumed in the USSR in 1955 and, while its share declined significantly, still made up some 28 percent in 1979. Exclusion of samogon from the per capita data would thus seriously understate the actual consumption of alcohol in the USSR.

In the late 1970s the USSR ranked seventh or eighth among some 30 countries[4] in consumption of alcohol (including samogon) per person fifteen years and older; without samogon the relative position of the USSR would drop to the thirteenth or fourteenth place.

An important characteristic of Soviet consumption of alcohol is the very high share of alcohol consumed in the form of strong beverages (40 percent of alcohol content and higher). International comparisons show that, as a rule, in countries with high per capita consumption of alcohol, most of it is consumed in the form of wine or beer, while in countries with relatively low per capita consumption most of alcohol is consumed in the form of strong beverages. In other words, per capita consumption of alcohol is inversely correlated with the share of strong beverages. For instance, Spearman rank correlation test applied to the consumption data for 26 countries (excluding the USSR) for the early 1970s [Hyman et al. 1980, p. 11] yields a coefficient of −0.87, indicating a strong inverse relationship.[5] Consumption of alcohol in the USSR is unique in this respect. In 1973 the share of strong beverages in the total consumption of alcohol in the USSR was 65 percent counting samogon and 55 percent excluding samogon compared with about 31 percent for 27 countries. The USSR thus ranked fourth in the share of strong beverages and eighth in consumption of alcohol per person fifteen years and older.

Another striking feature of the data presented in table 6.2 is the very high growth rate of per capita consumption of alcohol. The growth has been steady over the entire period and averaged 7.2 percent per annum for consumption of state-produced beverages and 4.4 percent per year if we were to add samogon to other beverages. For comparison purposes the data on consumption of alcohol per person fifteen years and older for the same period were collected for some 21 countries and the weighted average rate of growth was calculated as 2.7 percent per annum.[6] The average annual growth of consumption of alcohol in the USSR, regardless of whether samogon was counted or not, thus exceeded the average annual growth of 21 countries by a wide margin. Only Finland, Iceland, and Denmark recorded average annual rates of growth higher than the Soviet growth of 4.4 percent.

6.2. Regional Per Capita Consumption

Per capita consumption of alcohol in the USSR varies significantly by republic and region, and it appears that the ethnic composition of the region is one of the most important factors determining the alcohol consumption differentials. The author estimated per capita consumption of absolute alcohol by republic in an earlier study [Treml 1975, p. 298]. Since no new data were found to improve these estimates or to make estimates for a later year, the results are reproduced here without change (table 6.3).

Table 6.3. Per capita consumption of state-produced alcoholic beverages by Soviet republic, 1967, in liters of pure alcohol (Per person fifteen years old and older)

	Strong beverages	All beverages
USSR	5.00**	7.89**
RSFSR	6.32	9.07
Ukraine	3.12	6.16
Belorussia	4.35	6.71
Kazakhstan	5.46	8.59
Georgia	1.14	4.46
Azerbaidzhan	1.57	4.28
Lithuania	4.88	7.92
Moldavia	1.78	7.77
Latvia	5.63	8.94
Armenia	1.38	4.89
Estonia	6.21	10.23
Central-Asian Region*	2.13	4.53

*Turkmenistan, Tadzhikistan, Uzbekistan, and Kirgizia.
**The slight differences between USSR average per capita data here and in Table 6.1 are explained by probable error in the republican estimates.

The data exclude imported rum and wine, as well as domestically produced fruit and berry wines, and thus differ somewhat from estimates made in tables 2.5 and 6.1. The consumption of different beverages by type was estimated as follows.

Vodka and Vodka-type Beverages. For purposes of this study the consumption of vodka is equated to production, with some adjustments. This assumption is not too far-fetched. As a weight-gaining process the production of vodka is located close to the ultimate consumer [Vinogradov, ed., 1968, pp. 291–292; Kalobaev and Popov 1973, p. 212]. Zotov et al. [1967, p. 408] report that only 15 percent of the total output of vodka is transported by rail for an average distance of 394 km. In the 1960s only the Turkmen, Armenian and Azerbaidzhan republics did not have their own ethanol-processing plants [Pykhov 1966, p. 35].

Individual output estimates were derived as follows. RSFSR: Total output as reported in the republican handbook less 15 million liters exported to the Kazakh SSR [Zotov et al. 1967, p. 408]. Ukrainian and Lithuanian republics: As reported in republican handbooks. Belorussian, Moldavian, Estonian, Latvian and Azerbaidzhan republics: Output as estimated by interpolation and extrapolation of the data reported in republican handbooks for selected years (most often 1965 and 1970). Kazakh SSR: 1961 consumption of vodka estimated on the basis of turnover tax collection in Kazakhstan [Tulebaev 1963, p. 87] and the tax rate [Nazarian 1972, p. 24] as 76.7 million liters. The 1961–67 increase in sales of all alcoholic beverages was 1.68, about equal to the rate of increase in sales of alcoholic beverages nationally. But, as was pointed out above, sales of vodka were increasing somewhat more slowly. We thus used the national increase in vodka sales, or 1.45. Armenian SSR: In contrast to other republics Armenian sales of alcoholic beverages are reported by type, with 1964 the latest year available. Using total sales of vodka and its average price, the 1964 consumption is estimated at 3.3 million liters. The 1964–67 increase in total alcoholic beverage sales was 1.20, and the 1967 sales of vodka is thus estimated at about 4 million liters. Georgian SSR: The consumption of vodka in Georgia cannot be estimated directly but only through total sales data. First, the consistency of the estimates of consumption of alcoholic beverages in the two other Transcaucasian republics needs to be checked against ruble sales. We use 5.60 and 0.50 rubles per liter for vodka and beer, respectively, as these are standard national prices. Prices of wine, champagne, and cognac are somewhat lower as in a wine-growing zone and we use 8.07, 1.80 and 2.50 rubles per liter as prices of cognac, wine and champagne, respectively [Nazarian 1972, p. 26]. Using these prices and quantities estimated, we calculate total sales in the Azerbaidzhan and Armenian republics as 118 and 83 million rubles, respectively, compared with independently available estimates of 111 and 84 million rubles. The two estimates are sufficiently close to conclude that the method is acceptably accurate. Sale of vodka in Georgia was estimated as a residual by subtracting sales of vodka, beer, cognac, and champagne from the total value of sales of alcoholic beverages. By dividing this residual by an average price of one liter of vodka the estimated consumption of 8,566 million liters was obtained.

Wine (grape wine only). Estimates of the consumption of domestically produced wines are based on data reported by Shakhtan [1969, p. 280].

Beer. Shakhtan [1969, p. 288] has reported the beer-brewing capacities of the different republics as of January 1, 1967. Since his total of 3,849.9 million liters is fairly close to the domestic output of 3,614 million liters, we use his data. Beer, like vodka, is a weight-gaining commodity and shipments over long distances are quite small. The only republics which have been reported as beer exporters are Lithuania, Latvia, and Estonia. Since no data are available, no adjustments will be made.

Cognac. Consumption of cognac by republics is almost impossible to estimate accurately. One reason is that in contrast to other beverages, where imports constitute a small percentage of domestic production, about one third of the cognac consumed is imported. It must be noted, however, that cognac occupies a rather insignificant share in total consumption of absolute alcohol in the USSR: in 1967 it constituted only 2.5 percent. Thus, even a significant error in the estimates of its consumption would not materially affect the estimated regional consumption of alcohol.

All estimates of consumption are based on data reported by Shakhtan [1969, pp. 286–289]. The estimates for the Ukrainian, Moldavian, Georgian, Armenian and Azerbaidzhan republics are based on reported output, less exports to other republics, plus (only in the case of the RSFSR) imports from other republics. Similar data are not available for two groups of republics, the Baltic and the Central Asian. However, Shakhtan [1969, p. 285] reports per capita consumption of cognac in Estonia as the highest in the USSR (0.96 liter per capital) and the Uzbek SSR as the lowest (0.126 liter). We assume that these two republics are representative of their respective groups and estimate per capita consumption in Lithuania and Latvia at 0.9 liter and in Kirghiz, Tadzhik, Turkmen and Kazakh as 0.25 liter per capita. An average per capita consumption of 9.19 liters is used for the Belorussian republic. The estimates so made give us a total of 24,313 million liters of cognac out of the total consumption of 49,400 or a 24,313 million liter residual. The RSFSR is producing 5,787 thousand liters for a total consumption of 15,785 thousand liters of domestically produced cognac. We will assume that all of the residual of 24,313 thousand liters is consumed in the RSFSR. This is not unreasonable as it gives a per capita consumption of 0.19 or exactly the national per capita average.

Champagne. The estimates of champagne consumption for some republics are not very reliable but, as in the case of cognac, even significant error in some estimates would not materially affect overall results. The estimates were made as follow. According to Shakhtan [1969, p. 282] the RSFSR, Moldavian, Lithuanian, and Turkmen republics consumed approximately at the national per capita level of 0.224 liter. Using the average 1967 population, I estimate the total consumption in these four republics at some 30 million liters or about 57 percent of the total. The same source lists Georgia and the Kirghiz republics as consuming more than the national average, and the Ukraine, Azerbaidzhan, Armenia, Uzbek, Belorussia and Estonia as consuming less. As the first approximation we use 0.45 liter per capita as the best estimate for the first two, and 0.2 liter for the second group of six republics. For the three republics not mentioned in the source (Latvia, Tadzhik and Kazakh) the national estimate of 0.224 liter is used.

The figures in table 6.3 reflect average per capita consumption in republics and, because of the complex mix of different ethnic groups in the population, do not give the complete picture. We will take the analysis one step further and estimate per capita consumption of alcohol for three major groups which appear to have significantly different drinking habits: Muslims, Jews, and Slavs and other ethnic groups. Organized religion does not play a particularly important role in present day Soviet society, but the anti-alcohol dicta of Islam evidently still influence the drinking patterns of various ethnic groups which are or have been identified with Islam [Feshbach 1982 forthcoming]. Jews constitute another minority with a relatively low per capita consumption of alcohol. Judaic religion does not explicitly prohibit alcohol, as is the case with Islam, but custom and tradition did make the Jews moderate drinkers. The estimates made here are based on a rather strong assumption that the per capita consumption of each of the three groups is identical regardless of the area where the group lives.

Since reliable statistics for age and ethnic structure of the Soviet population are available only for the census year we will use 1970 data. The per capita figures given above were advanced to 1970 on the basis of sales of alcoholic beverages by republic in constant prices and the 1967–1970 changes in the population of persons fifteen years and older. The population of all fifteen republics was broken down into Muslims, Jews, and Slavs and other ethnic groups (see table 6.7). Thus, for each republic we could write the following equation:

$$P_s a_s + P_m a_m + P_j a_j = P_t a_t$$

where
  P stands for the population
  a stands for average per capita consumption of absolute alcohol per person fifteen years and older
  s (subscript) stands for Slavs
  j (subscript) stands for Jews
  m (subscript) stands for Muslims
  t (subscript) stands for total for the given republic.

Solving these equations and averaging the results gave us the following per capita figures in liters of absolute alcohol: Slavs and other ethnic groups, excluding Muslims and Jews, 9.44; Muslims, 4.72; Jews, 5.01. It must be stressed that these figures are just first approximations because of the absence of accurate population statistics and because of probable errors in the alcohol data by republic. Thus, for instance, the difference between alcohol consumption of Muslims and Jews may be statistically insignificant.

It must be emphasized that the data on regional consumption of alcoholic beverages and the derived measures of per capita consumption by ethnic groups refer only to state produced beverages. Consumption of home-distilled samogon and of other homemade beverages such as grape and fruit wines, beer, and braga contributes significantly to the total per capita consumption. (See chapter 5). However, only samogon and homemade grape wine production can be estimated with any degree of accuracy. In the late 1960s and early 1970s consumption of these homemade beverages can be roughly estimated at over 4 liters of absolute alcohol per person fifteen years and older.

Production and consumption of homemade beverages is also highly differentiated by regions and ethnic groups. Thus, the three major Slavic republics, the RSFSR, the Ukraine, and Belorussia, probably account for some 95 percent of samogon. Homemaking of grape wine is concentrated in Moldavia, Georgia, the Ukraine, and Uzbekistan, while fruit and berry wines are made in the Ukraine, Belorussia, and Georgia. Unfortunately, it is virtually impossible to estimate production of these beverages by republic and to correct the per capita data shown in table 6.3. However, using some rather tenuous assumptions and approximations it was estimated that in the early 1970s Muslims and Jews consumed between one-fourth and one-third of the amount of alcohol consumed by Slavs if both state-produced and homemade beverages are included.

The regional differences in per capita consumption of absolute alcohol discussed above are for 1970 and estimation for later years is impossible because of the lack of the necessary data. However as a proxy for consumption of absolute alcohol in liters we can use the data on expenditures on alcoholic beverages. In 1970–1979 the growth of expenditures on alcoholic beverages in constant prices per person fifteen years old and older has been estimated as 1.08 for Kazkhstan, Azerbaidzhan, and Central Asia, and 1.13 for the rest of the USSR. The rates of change over time have been sufficiently different for us to conclude that the differences in drinking among Slavs and Muslims have been increasing since 1970.

6.3. *Expenditures on Alcohol in Consumers' Budgets*

As the result of high per capita consumption of alcoholic beverages and of prices which are high relative to incomes, Soviet consumers spend an extraordinarily large share of their budgets on alcohol. Accurate measurement and analysis of the relationship between alcohol expenditures and consumers' budgets are difficult, because of the absence of the necessary data; we have to estimate new series and use indirect evidence.

Soviet sources offer several studies of consumers' family budgets based on large sample surveys; while as a rule alcohol expenditures are not identified separately there are some exceptions. Thus, a massive statistical study of workers' family budgets in several regions in Siberia in the 1946–1957 period indicates that alcoholic beverages constituted on the average some 3.4 percent of all expenditures [Alexeev and Bukin 1980 pp. 66–81]. A study, which was probably done in the late 1970s, of 863 families of different social background in an unnamed Siberian town shows an average expenditure on alcohol of 6.6 percent [Rimashevskaia and Ovsiannikov 1981, pp. 1091–1094]. The problem with these and similar budget studies is that alcohol expenditures are much too low relative to other expenditures in the light of what we generally know about sales of alcoholic beverages and average incomes in the USSR.

The explanation of the observed discrepancy is found in a special Gosplan study of the structure of workers' and kolkhozniks' expenditures in the 1953–1968 period. The authors of the study compared the structures of expenditures derived from family surveys with retail trade statistics and found the two sets of data basically consistent, except that expenditures on alcohol based on family surveys were on the average 2.5 times lower than the retail trade data and that expenditures on food were correspondingly higher [Maier and Ershov, eds. 1971, p. 87].[7] The authors concluded that the respondents have consistently understated expenditures on alcohol in their reporting. With continuous antidrinking campaigns and official condemnation of alcohol abuse in the USSR, this bias in reporting is not surprising. A comparison of survey-based expenditure data for Siberian regions, referred to earlier, with the available retail sales data reveals a possible understatement of alcohol expenditures in the former.[8] Since we have no reason to suspect an upward bias in retail trade statistics we have to conclude that Soviet respondents to budget questionnaires have a persistent tendency to understate the reported expenditures on alcohol.

In the absence of statistics on absolute levels of the distribution of personal incomes in the USSR, we will use several different measures to relate expenditures on alcoholic beverages and incomes. An important caveat must be noted at this point. The people of the USSR are entitled to free medical and educational services and, as a rule, spend little on housing which is heavily subsidized by the state. Thus, the pattern of personal expenditures differs significantly from that in the West and direct comparisons can be somewhat misleading. The significant increase in expenditures on alcohol (without illegal home-produced beverages) relative to incomes is perhaps best illustrated by changes in expenditures juxtaposed to changes in wages in the USSR (see table 6.4).

We will use the recently published CIA series on Soviet disposable money income as the basis for estimating the share of expenditures on alcoholic beverages in consumer's budgets. The CIA study calculates disposable money income as the sum of wages, net money income from sales of farm products, military pay and allowances, interest on savings, and transfer payments less direct taxes, dues, and state loans [Denton 1979 pp. 785–789]. The share of expenditures on state-produced alcoholic beverages in current prices (tables 3.3 and 3.9) of total disposable income were calculated as follows: 1955, 12.8 percent; 1960, 13.3 percent; 1965, 13.8 percent; 1970, 15.3 percent; 1975, 14.7 percent; 1977, 15.0 percent.[9]

As was discussed in chapter 5, Soviet drinkers consume large quantities of illegal home-produced alcoholic beverages such as samogon, grape and fruit wines, beer, and braga. In the late 1970s the total cost of these beverages, valued at average black market prices, can be roughly estimated at 9–11 billion rubles. Theft of alcohol from various alcohol and vodka-producing industries and of industrial alcohol and alcohol-containing fluids is practiced on a large scale in the USSR, and some of this alcohol finds its way into the black market. Although it is very difficult to estimate the values involved they must be significant.

A major additional expenditure incurred by Soviet drinkers is in premiums paid for alcoholic beverages purchased through middlemen during restricted hours or in restricted areas. Of the 533 Soviet émigré families surveyed in the Second Economy project, 89 or 17 percent of the total reported having annually purchased on the average some 14 liters of vodka through middlemen. Rough calculations indicate that the premiums paid over the state retail price amounted to some 600–700 million rubles in the late 1970s.

Another group of personal expenditures which should be accounted for are the various costs related to the effects of drinking and alcohol abuse such as medical expenses of treatment of alcoholics and fines and charges levied against drunkards. Most of these costs are impossible to estimate but they must be quite high. As one example, we can mention the network of sobering-up stations maintained by the police for overnight confinement of arrested drunkards. According to one recent

Table 6.4. Alcohol expenditure and average wages, rubles

	Annual expenditure on alcohol per person fifteen years old and older	Average annual wage of workers and employees
1955	50.87	858
1965	97.98	1,158
1979	201.03	1,960
1979 over 1955	3.95	2.28

Soviet source, between 12 and 15 percent of the adult population of the USSR end up in sobering-up stations annually [Lulochkin 1981, p. 136]. With the average charge of 30 rubles per visit (a 15 ruble fine and a 15 ruble charge for services) the total cost would range from 550 to 800 million rubles, depending on whether the author referred to the total or the urban population.

Accurate estimates of these expenditures are impossible but the inclusion of some of the additional elements mentioned above would bring the share of expenditure on alcohol to over 20 percent of disposable money income.[10] In the 1970s in most industrial nations consumers were spending between 3 and 6 percent of their household budgets on alcoholic beverages [Schroeder and Edwards 1981, pp. 23–24]; the Soviet ratio of 15–20 percent is exceptionally high by international standards. Aside from the known negative effects of alcohol abuse and heavy drinking, high expenditures on alcoholic beverages pose an important question concerning the welfare of low- and middle-income Soviet families which spend a higher than average share of their household budgets on alcohol. Unfortunately, our analysis cannot be extended much beyond this point because of an almost complete absence of Soviet statistics on income distribution and the distribution of expenditures on alcoholic beverages by different income groups in the USSR.

In a recently completed major study, Alistair McAuley demonstrated that in the mid-and late-1960s the distribution of earnings and of personal incomes in the USSR displayed a marked degree of inequality and that a large segment of the Soviet population lives below the poverty line, which is defined by Soviet statisticians as 50 rubles per month per capita [1979, pp. 3–7, and pp. 56–88]. Several experimental tests were run with actual Soviet wage and alcohol expenditure statistics and under varying assumptions concerning population parameters, relationship between income and consumption of alcohol, and frequency distribution of family expenditures on alcoholic beverages. The purpose of these tests was to ascertain the number of Soviet families who spend an arbitrarily chosen 40 percent or more of their budgets on alcohol.

For income statistics, McAuley's frequency distributions of family income for the urban (nonagricultural) population in 1967 and of kolkhoznik families in 1968 were used [1979, pp. 56–66]; that is, sovkhoz families and all urban and rural single individuals were omitted. The basis statistics used in tests were as shown in table 6.5.

Table 6.5. Basic statistics, urban and kolkhoznik families

	Urban families	Kolkhoznik families
	1967	1968
Total number of families (millions)	32.3	12.7
Size of the family	3.71	4.10
Number of adults per family	2.66	2.69
Expenditures on state-produced alcoholic beverages, per adult, rubles per year	150.6	69.8
Expenditures on "samogon" included on both income and expenditure side	excluded	51.5

In the absence of any Soviet statistics, the frequency distribution of expenditures on alcoholic beverages derived from a sample survey of 533 recent Soviet émigré families was used. Several Western studies showed that the frequency distribution of per capita consumption of alcohol in different societies and cultures tends to be log-normal (i.e. skewed to the right), relatively smooth, and fairly similar in terms of main parameters [de Lint 1973, pp. 75–108]. The frequency distribution derived from the émigré sample fits very well into the general international pattern and its use for the entire Soviet population seems to be justified, at least on an experimental basis. The émigré data refer to the mid- and late-1970s and were obtained from a group the majority of whom were moderately drinking Jews. Therefore the distribution was converted from absolute rubles to percentages of the average expenditures on alcoholic beverages. The original distribution is reproduced in table 6.6.

The distribution was then applied to each of the income groups shown in McAuley's tables; that is, it was assumed that expenditures on alcoholic beverages and the parameters of the distribution of per capita alcohol expenditures are independent of family income.[11]

It must be pointed out that one specific characteristic of the émigré-derived distribution of alcohol expenditures could not have been adjusted for. There is some evidence that, as a rule, the frequency distribution of per capita consumption of alcohol is more peaked (has a more pronounced kurtosis) in societies with a lower consumption of alcohol [de Lint 1973, pp. 76–77]. Both because of the dominant role of Jews in the sample and because the émigré data refer to the mid- and late-1970s, when per capita consumption of alcohol in the USSR was higher than in the mid-1960s, we can assume that the émigré-based frequency distribution is more peaked than the true frequency distribution for the entire Soviet population in 1967–1968.

It can be shown, for two populations identical in size and in per capita expenditures on alcohol, that the population with a more peaked frequency distribution

Table 6.6. Distribution of expenditure on alcoholic beverages

Rubles per month per person fifteen years old and over	Percent of the sample group
0	3.20
0.01– 4.99	24.11
5.00– 9.99	35.22
10.00–14.99	19.77
15.00–19.99	6.59
20.00–24.99	2.83
25.00–29.99	3.39
30.00–34.99	1.32
35.00–39.99	0.75
40.00–44.99	0.38
45.00–49.99	0.38
50.00–54.99	1.13
55.00–59.99	0.38
60.00 and over	0.57

(For the grouped data the mean is 10.91 rubles, the median 8.24 rubles, the mode 7.25 rubles, standard deviation 12.22 rubles, and the Pearson's measure of skewness 0.30.)

will have a lower number of people spending in excess of the given percent of their budgets on alcohol. Thus, the use of a more peaked frequency distribution for the purposes of this analysis introduced a downward bias in the results, i.e. led to an understatement of the number spending in excess of 40 percent of their family incomes on alcohol. However, other assumptions and simplifications used in the tests conceivably introduced an upward bias. The assumption that the distribution of per capita expenditures on alcohol is identical within each income group is in all probability incorrect and would tend to overstate the number of families spending in excess of 40 percent of their income on alcohol. It is to be hoped that the two biases have at least partially cancelled each other.

The tests showed that in 1967 between 8 and 9 percent or between 2.6 and 2.9 million urban families spent 40 percent of their family budgets or more on state-produced alcoholic beverages, and that of this number between 1.6 and 2.3 million families were below the poverty line of 50 rubles per month per member. A different way of looking at the impact of excessive drinking is this. According to McAuley, in 1967 32.5 percent of all urban families had incomes of less than 50 rubles per month. If we were to accept the Soviet position that 50 rubles is the minimal amount of income necessary to maintain a socially-acceptable standard of living, then we must conclude that some 3.4–3.5 million urban families with incomes higher than the minimum were pushed below the poverty line by their excessive consumption of alcohol.[12]

In 1968 between 10 and 11 percent or between 1.3 and 1.4 million kolkhoznik families spent 40 percent of their family budgets or more on purchases of state-produced alcoholic beverages and samogon.[13] Of this number between 7.5 and 8 percent or between 0.9 and 1.0 million families were below the poverty line. These conclusions pertain to the entire country. It is quite clear that since per capita expenditures on alcohol differ by a factor of 2 or more in different republics the financial burden of drinking must be particularly high among the heavy-drinking Slavs and Baltic nationalities.

Unfortunately, the absence of Soviet data made it impossible for McAuley to extend his analysis to later years. In all probability the degree of income inequality in the USSR was somewhat reduced between the mid-1960s and the late-1970s. However, since per capita expenditure on alcoholic beverages in this period was increasing faster than incomes we can conjecture that the financial burden of drinking did not become any lighter since the mid-1960s. It must be emphasized that the shortcomings of the underlying data, the gross simplifications, and the tenuous assumptions used in the analysis make the conclusions at best first approximations. However, the order of magnitude is probably roughly correct and the main conclusions are valid.

For most countries and societies the disposable or the "after tax" income is an acceptable measure of welfare. However, for a country such as the USSR where, depending on definitions, expenditures on alcohol reach a level between 15 and 20 percent of the average disposable income, a measure of "after tax and after alcohol" income seems to be more appropriate. Needless to say, other societies have "skid row" individuals and families which find themselves in financial difficulties because of alcoholism. However, in societies in which the expenditures on alcohol make up 3–6 percent of an average family budget, the number of such families would be rather small. On the other hand, in the USSR the combined effect of high consumption of alcohol and of prices of alcoholic beverages which are very high relative to incomes places several million low-income families in extremely difficult financial situations. A Soviet low- or even a middle-income family allocating 40 or more percent of its budget to alcohol must live in abject misery. This dimension of the poverty issue in the USSR has been neglected in both Western and Soviet sources.

As was mentioned earlier per capita consumption of alcohol in the USSR is highly differentiated by republics and ethnic groups.[14] Per capita consumption of alcohol is not identical with per capita expenditure on alcoholic beverages because of price differences and other factors, but, as a rule they are fairly close. It should therefore be stressed that the figures given above reflect national averages and that the shares of family budget spent on alcoholic beverages vary significantly by republic.

We do not have the necessary information on disposable income by republic. However, we can get a good idea of differences in alcohol expenditures by using the 1970 personal income statistics prepared by McAuley [1979, p. 109]. Table 6.7 reproduces McAuley's personal income data by republics with one modification—the per capita income figures were recomputed to reflect personal income per person fifteen years and older to allow a more meaningful comparison with expenditures on alcoholic beverages per person fifteen years and older. It would have been

Table 6.7. Personal income and expenditures on alcoholic beverages per person 15 years and older, by republics, 1970,* rubles per year

	Personal income	Expenditures on alcohol	Share of expenditures on alcohol in personal income (percent)
USSR	1,124	146.5	13.0
RSFSR	1,174	185.9	15.8
Ukraine	1,033	108.2	10.5
Belorussia	1,054	119.9	11.4
Uzbekistan	1,078	92.3	8.6
Kazakhstan	1,118	164.1	14.7
Georgia	1,027	65.1	6.3
Azerbaidzhan	942	61.3	6.5
Lithuania	1,289	141.9	11.0
Moldavia	1,012	86.5	8.5
Latvia	1,276	179.1	14.0
Kirgizia	933	131.1	13.2
Tadzhikistan	941	65.0	6.9
Armenia	1,145	74.9	6.5
Turkmenistan	1,142	104.7	9.2
Estonia	1,365	189.4**	13.9

*Personal income data from McAuley, 1979, p. 109 converted to income per person 15 years old and older. Expenditures on alcoholic beverages include public dining markup.
**Estonia is the only Soviet republic for which sales of "other foods" including alcoholic beverages have not been published since the early 1960s. The value used here is a rough estimate.

preferable to calculate family incomes and expenditures, but we do not have sufficient demographic data. The last column in table 6.7 must thus serve as a proxy for the share of alcohol expenditures in family budgets. The data exclude consumption of samogon and other home-produced beverages which cannot be calculated by republics. Rather rough estimates indicate that alcohol expenditures in the RSFSR, the Ukraine, Belorussia and Moldavia would have been much higher were we able to account for home-produced beverages.

7. Population of the USSR

7.1 Population Series for Persons Fifteen Years Old and Older

The various population series used in this study are summarized in table 7.1. The data for the total USSR population and the population fifteen years and older are from FDAD [1973, pp. 20–21] and FDAD [1979, p. 25]. The breakdown of the population of all ages into urban and rural population is based on percentages regularly published in standard statistical sources.

Accurate data for the urban-rural breakdown for the population fifteen years and older are available only for the 1959 and the 1970 census years. The shares of population fifteen years and older in total population in urban and rural areas appear to be fairly constant (see table 7.2).

Thus, the ratio of urban adults to the total adult population is somewhat higher than the ratio of the urban population of all ages to the total population. The difference is 4.03 percentage points in 1959 and 5.88 percentage points in 1970. It was assumed that the difference was changing linearly over the period under consideration. The adult population in urban areas was then estimated by applying the urban-total percentage for the population of all ages (column 2 ÷ column 1) times the adjustment factor to the population fifteen years and older.

Estimation of the urban and rural population fifteen years and older for the 1971–1978 period presents a problem. The preliminary results of the 1979 census published so far do not include the age distribution by urban and rural areas, but only the totals. The estimates will be made on the basis of the 1970 census data on age, sex, area of residence, and the series on the male-female composition of the population fifteen years and older provided by the FDAD. We will start with the following data (see table 7.3).

Using these ratios we will estimate the adjustment factor necessary to move the 1970 ratio to the 1979 level.

$$\text{adjustment factor for males} = \frac{M_{79}^t}{(r_{79}^m)(M_{70}^u) + (1 - r_{79}^m)(M_{70}^r)} \ .$$

That is, we assume that the age structure of the population by sex and area of residence remains constant and that the overall ratios change only because of changes in the rural-urban and male-female ratios. The adjustment factors so calculated are for males = 1.0685, for females = 1.0445.

Using the adjustment factors we can calculate the ratio of males and females aged fifteen and older by area of residence (see table 7.4). Applying these ratios to the reported 1979 census subtotals we estimate urban population as 65.51 percent and rural population as 34.49 percent. The 1971–1978 estimates were made by interpolation.

Table 7.1. Population of the USSR (urban and rural), millions as of mid-year

	Population of all ages			Population 15 Years old and older		
	Total	Urban	Rural	Total	Urban	Rural
1955	196.2	87.3	108.9	141.3	65.1	76.2
1956	199.7	89.9	109.8	144.0	67.2	76.8
1957	203.2	93.4	109.8	145.9	69.6	76.3
1958	206.8	98.2	108.6	146.7	72.4	74.3
1959	210.5	102.1	108.4	147.4	74.4	73.0
1960	214.3	106.1	108.2	148.4	76.5	71.9
1961	218.1	110.1	108.0	149.9	78.9	71.0
1962	221.7	113.1	108.6	151.9	81.0	70.9
1963	225.1	115.9	109.2	154.2	83.1	71.1
1964	228.1	119.8	108.3	156.8	86.3	70.5
1965	230.9	122.4	108.5	159.5	88.7	70.8
1966	233.5	124.9	108.6	162.3	91.3	71.0
1967	236.0	128.6	107.4	165.0	94.7	70.3
1968	238.3	131.1	107.2	167.6	97.3	70.3
1969	240.6	133.5	107.1	170.3	99.9	70.4
1970	242.8	137.2	105.6	173.1	103.6	69.5
1971	245.1	140.9	104.2	176.2	107.5	68.7
1972	247.5	143.7	103.8	179.2	110.6	68.6
1973	249.7	147.0	102.8	182.4	114.4	68.0
1974	252.1	150.2	101.9	185.5	118.0	67.5
1975	254.4	153.5	101.0	188.7	121.8	66.9
1976	256.8	156.5	100.3	191.7	125.3	66.4
1977	259.0	159.3	99.7	194.5	128.6	65.9
1978	261.3	162.1	99.2	197.0	131.7	65.3
1979	263.4	164.4	99.0	199.1	134.2	64.9

Table 7.2. Urban population of the USSR as percentage of total

	For all ages	For ages 15 and over
1959	47.88	49.81
1970	56.26	59.57

7.2 Distribution of the Population by Ethnic Groups

Separation of the population of the USSR into Muslims, Jews, and Slavs and other ethnic groups, shown in table 7.5, was done in several steps.

Soviet demographic sources do not identify ethnic groups by present or historical religious affiliation (such as Muslim). Thus, as the first step, the Muslim population of all fifteen republics was estimated on the basis of the 1970 population census data for population of all ages by republic and ethnic-religious affiliation

Table 7.3. Percentage of population fifteen years and older in total

M^u_{70}	1970 male urban population	72.7
M^r_{70}	1970 male rural population	61.8
M^t_{79}	1979 total male population	73.3
F^u_{70}	1970 female urban population	77.4
F^r_{70}	1970 female rural population	68.9
F^t_{79}	1979 female total population	77.5
r^m_{79}	1979 ratio of urban to rural males of all ages	(62.39) : (37.61)
r^f_{79}	1979 ratio of urban to rural females of all ages	(62.31) : (37.69)

Table 7.4. Percentage of total of the given sex and area

1979 male urban population	77.68
1979 male rural population	66.03
1979 female urban population	80.84
1979 female rural population	71.97

Table 7.5. Distribution of the Soviet population by ethnicity/religion, 1970

	Total population	Slavs and other ethnic groups	Muslims	Jews
USSR	171,696.9	150,890.7	18,879.2	1,927.0
RSFSR	95,608.1	89,474.2	5,410.0	723.9
Ukraine	35,391.6	34,695.3	0	696.3
Belorussia	6,400.4	6,267.8	0	132.6
Uzbekistan	6,478.2	1,328.2	5,057.8	92.2
Kazakhstan	8,130.6	5,165.7	2,940.1	24.8
Georgia	3,252.1	2,953.5	249.0	49.6
Azerbaidzhan	2,860.4	688.7	2,134.7	37.0
Lithuania	2,280.3	2,259.2	0	21.1
Moldavia	2,423.4	2,335.5	0	87.9
Latvia	1,853.4	1,820.5	0	32.9
Kirgizia	1,709.9	839.0	864.0	6.9
Tadzhikistan	1,548.6	313.2	1,222.3	13.1
Armenia	1,512.6	1,412.6	99.1	.9
Turkmenistan	1,189.6	284.3	902.2	3.1
Estonia	1,057.7	1,053.0	0	4.7

given in Rapawy [1980]. In a few cases, when an ethnic group was given as Christian/Muslim, an arbitrary 50-50 division was effected. The residuals of unidentified ethnic groups in each republic was divided into Muslims and Slavs in proportion to their respective shares in the identified segment of the population. The number of Jews was listed as published. The population of all ages was converted into the population of persons fifteen years and older as follows. Jewish population for all republics was estimated on the basis of the age structure of the Jewish population of the RSFSR—the only republic for which it is available. The age distribution of the Muslim population was determined directly from the census data when available and on the basis of average structure when not available. The age structure of Slavs was estimated as a residual.

Notes

1. Production and Supply of Alcoholic Beverages in the Soviet Union

1. The output of beer in 1980 which is not shown in table 1.1 was reported as 6,130 million liters, which is about 10 percent lower than the peak output of 1978.

2. Calculated based on the average requirement of 0.168 kg of barley malt per liter of beer [Balashov 1979, p. 75] and statistics on malt imports.

3. Based on published import statistics and the requirement for hops estimated at 0.0021 kg per liter [Balashov 1979, pp. 74–75].

3. State Trade in Alcoholic Beverages: Prices, Sales and Taxes

1. According to various reports, prices for alcoholic beverages in open state stores are between 1.5 and 4 times higher than in hard currency stores [Radio Liberty CRD 355/70 October 6, 1970, T3T9-74KK, T3T4-76EE].

2. The author visited several Moscow stores in January 1981, and found only three brands of relatively expensive vodkas: "Russkaia," priced at 8.84 rubles per liter, "Pshenichnaia," at 10.67, and "Sibirskaia," at 12.00. Inquiries about less expensive brands produced the standard answer: "We have not seen them for over a year."

3. Prices of both vodka products and wines were raised some 20 percent in 1958. As a result, sales of wines decreased and the authorities hastened to rescind increases in wine prices in 1959 [Stoliarov 1969, pp. 113–114].

4. In 1972 some 73 percent of all turnover taxes was levied in consumer goods [Gallik et al. Table A-11]. The structure of turnover taxes probably did not change much and the same rate is applied to 1979 total tax collections of 88.3 billion rubles.

5. For instance, in 1975 the total value of imported alcoholic beverages was 380 million rubles. Pricing these beverages at average domestic prices net of turnover taxes yields an estimated value of domestic sales of over 1,200 million rubles.

6. In an earlier study the author suggested that the Soviet government has little leeway in the pursuit of antidrinking policies. Any drastic cut in sales of alcoholic beverages would result in reductions in state revenues and in significant imbalances between expenditures and incomes of the population. Thus, any radical antidrinking measure would have to be accompanied by far-reaching fiscal and price reforms [Treml 1975, pp. 161–177].

4. Production and use of Ethanol

1. The output index for the ethanol sector of the food industry is available for all years but cannot be applied directly, because the industry is producing a variety of products in addition to ethanol. Another problem lies with the exact coverage of the index—it seems that the sector covers food-based as well as sulfite and hydrolytic ethanol, but in the absence of a published sector definition we cannot be certain.

2. The consumption of grain products is reported in terms of flour which was converted to grain on the basis of a coefficient of 0.79 tons of flour per ton of grain [Zotov et al. eds., 1967, p. 288].

3. All of the information found in technical sources as well as the empirical evidence suggest that only wood-hydrolytic alcohol was or still is used for human consumption. Of the 56 recent Soviet émigrés who answered this question in the "Second Economy" émigré survey, 41 reported the use of wood-hydrolytic alcohol and only 15 indicated the use of alcohol made from oil or gas, i.e., ethylene-based. Thus it seems that Khrushchev was in error referring to vodka made out of natural gas but, of course, this possibility cannot be completely rejected.

4. In 1963–1964 the USSR imported an average of about 6,000,000 tons of grain, compared with average 1955–1962 imports of 350,000 tons.

5. Production of Samogon and other Homemade Beverages

1. Samogon (literally: "self-distilled") is the Russian slang term for an alcoholic beverage varying in alcohol content from 25 to 50 percent and distilled from the commodities listed. Synonymous slang terms are "pervach" (literally: first batch in the brewing process) or "sivukha" (derived from the Russian word for fusel oils). In addition to samogon a variety of strong homemade beverages are associated with ethnic minorities such as "chacha" or "tutovaia vodka" (Caucasus) or "araka" (Soviet Central Asia). We will use samogon as a generic term describing all strong home-distilled beverages.

2. The absence of any information on samogon production at republican or oblast' levels is illustrated in reports in Shumskii 1973, p. 6, and ABSEES, January 1973.

3. To simplify the presentation of making estimates, only the independent data (Table 5.2) and the final results (Table 5.1) will be offered here.

4. I am particularly grateful to Professor Peter Wiles of the London School of Economics who strongly argued with me about the large-scale distillation of samogon in Soviet cities.

5. In fact, one knowledgeable émigré from one of the Baltic republics insisted that by the mid-1970s samogon was produced almost exclusively in cities [G1G 10−80 AB]. The explanation of this statement, which contradicts all other available evidence, lies possibly in the population mix. A significant share of the population of the Baltic republics consists of Russians and other Slavs, who concentrate mainly in urban areas and are practically absent from rural areas. If Slavs are more disposed towards samogon than the Baltic nationalities samogon production in cities may indeed exceed that in the rural areas.

6. Of 464 émigrés who answered the question in the "Second Economy" survey 346 reported that samogon is made of sugar or of sugar and other commodities, and 118 said that samogon is made from products other than sugar.

7. Some émigré reports indicate that relatively sophisticated equipment is used by some home brewers. The low rate of output of alcohol per kg of sugar in home brewing, however, stems primarily from small batches of output. This feature of samogon production has not changed since the 1920s.

8. Total consumption of sugar is from standard U.S. statistical sources. Direct consumption of sugar was calculated on the basis of U.S. input-output tables for 1947, 1963, 1967 and 1972 and the relevant price data. Per capita consumption by different income groups in the U.S. is available only in terms of combined consumption of sugar and sweets. These data show only small fluctuations among households with different incomes in the 1940−1950s.

9. The Ukraine and Belorussia are shown separately from the RSFSR because we do not have the data for urban-rural breakdown for the latter after 1967.

10. A certain share of sugar may be used in rural areas for productive purposes other than samogon distillation—for instance, for the making of fruit and berry preserves or homemade wines for sale in urban *kolkhoz* markets. However, the USSR is not a major producer of fruits—in the early 1970s, between 4 and 5 million tons of fruits and berries (excluding grapes) were retained by rural growers, i.e., were left after state procurement. Out of this quantity significant amounts were consumed fresh, sold fresh in urban markets, and consumed in rural areas in the form of preserves or beverages. It should also be pointed out that, as a rule, prices of fresh fruits in urban kolkhoz markets are fairly high, while the state retail trade network offers sufficiently large quantities of canned fruits and preserves to make urban sales of homemade preserves less financially attractive than sales of fresh fruits.

11. Two factors probably contribute to an overstatement of the per capita consumption of sugar in Moscow. In the first place, a large number of visitors (both tourists and officials) must consume a certain share of sugar. Secondly, a certain share of sugar is used in the production of samogon. Thus, the true consumption which can be considered as representing a saturation point would fall within the 22−26 kg range suggested above.

12. In contrast to the average of 160 liters confiscated per arrest in the USSR, in the US the average quantity of liquor and mash seized per illegal still in the late 1970s was 1,235 liters [Hyman et al. 1980, p. 10].

13. The terms "braga" and "brazhka" are used in a number of different ways in modern Russian. "Brazhka" means the fermenting mesh from which samogon will be distilled but can be also used to denote a relatively mild (1.5 to 8 percent alcohol) beverage prepared from grain, flour, or bread with added sugar and yeast but without distillation. "Braga" usually means a mild beverage (1.5 to 5 percent alcohol) made from bread, sugar, and yeast.

14. Until 1969 gross output of grapes by kolkhozes and sovkhozes exceeded the state procurement. As a first approximation, we will assume that kolkhozes and sovkhozes retained some grapes and that private growers did not deliver any grapes to the state. Starting in 1969, state procurement of grapes has been

larger than the gross output of kolkhozes and sovkhozes, suggesting that some grapes were procured from private growers. Under the circumstances we will estimate grapes retained by private growers as equal to their gross output in the 1955–1968 period and adjust the output downward by the difference between the gross output of the state sector and state procurement for the 1969–1979 period.

15. No data on the production ratios in home manufacture of fruit and berry wines were found in the literature. The ratios given above are approximate estimates based on the output of alcohol in the form of samogon from fruits and berries [Cherliunchakevich 1929, pp. 38–39].

16. Indirect evidence supporting this statement is seen in the very rapid expansion of production of pressed (baking) yeast in the USSR, which increased 3.7 times in the 1955–1979 period [Zotov 1958, p. 96; "Razvitie" 1980, pp. 6–8]. In the same period production of flour and the output of state bakeries increased by only some 35–40 percent. Production of yeast thus appears to be far in excess of legitimate needs of baking and of other uses as the excess supply is used in samogon distillation, and production of homemade fruit and berry wines, beer, and braga.

6. Per Capita Consumption of Alcohol in the USSR

1. Some of the alcohol stolen from places of employment has already been counted. Thus, beverages produced and supplied to the trade organizations have been included in the total supply estimates made in this study. However, most thefts reported in the Soviet media are from industrial enterprises, construction, and medical organizations using alcohol for technical purposes. Of the 81 émigrés, who reported taking alcohol from their places of employment, only 9 were employed in trade. Thus, in all probability, a large share of stolen alcohol should be added to total consumption.

2. Based on the standard Soviet retirement ages of 60 for men, 55, for women, and the population data for 1960 from FDAD 1973, pp. 23–26.

3. The assumptions used in this analysis, such as the age intervals actually used in the Gosplan study or the year for which the data were given, are not particularly important. Thus, varying the age groups, or changing the base year from 1960 to 1965, does not change the conclusions.

4. The per capita data for some 30–40 countries used in this section were culled from several sources [Efron et al. 1974, pp. 10–11, Hyman et al. 1980, p. 11, and Partanen 1981, p. 181]. The last source reproduced the data from a 1975 study of the Finnish Foundation for Alcohol Studies which was not available to this author. These data are particularly valuable as they cover the 1950–1952 period. For statistics for the late 1970s the data compiled by the British Wine and Spirit Association, published in the *London Times* [August 20, 1981, p. 3], were used. Compared with the estimate of Soviet per capita consumption of 9.0 liters made in this study the *London Times*'article shows 6.2 liters, which is considered to be in error and rejected. Otherwise, the *Times*'data appear reasonable compared with other sources and are used here for the late 1970s. The list of the countries included in the comparison covers most of Western Europe, the US, Canada, Australia, and Japan. Unfortunately, no comparable data are available for most countries of Asia, Latin America and Africa.

5. Spearman rank correlation coefficient is calculated as

$$= 1 - \frac{6 \Sigma d^2}{N^3 - N}$$

where d stands for the absolute difference in the rankings of phenomena being tested and N stands for the size of the sample. The coefficient of rank correlation ranges from + 1.0 for perfect **rank** correspondence to 0 for no correlation, to −1.0 for perfect inverse rank correspondence.

6. The beginning of the period over which the average rate of growth was calculated, differed depending on the country from 1950–1952 and 1955. Average annual rates of growth were calculated separately for all 21 countries and then averaged using 1973 population statistics as weights.

7. Expenditures on food in family surveys were overstated by 13 percent which, in ruble terms, corresponded to the understatement of alcohol expenditures by a factor of 2.5. We have verified this statement of Soviet authors by comparing expenditures on alcohol with expenditures on food estimated as the sum of retail trade, urban farmers' market sales, and consumption in kind, with the latter two elements taken from Denton 1979, p. 766. Indeed, on the average in the 1953–1968 period, 13 percent of food expenditures was equal to 60 percent of alcohol expenditures, i.e. $(1 - 1/2.5)$.

8. The Siberian survey data were presented in terms of ruble expenditures on alcohol and other goods per average family. The ratios of alcohol expenditures to expenditures on food and soft goods were calculated and compared with similar ratios derived from retail trade statistics for six cities and regions in

1957. In all cases the ratios derived from retail trade statistics were approximately twice as high as the ratios based on family budgets, suggesting that alcohol expenditures were understated, or food and soft goods expenditures overstated, in family surveys. The former conclusion is, of course, more likely.

9. Denton's study is carried only through 1977.

10. In order to properly account for illegally produced beverages and premiums paid to middlemen, the ruble values must be added both to expenditures and to the income, as these elements constitute income to a certain segment of the population. The figure of 20 percent given is based on income data adjusted in this manner.

11. A series of regression tests applied to the émigré survey data indicated no statistically significant correlation between net wages of the family and expenditures on alcoholic beverages either per adult or per family. Data on income elasticity of demand for alcoholic beverages would have been extremely helpful for this phase of our study. Unfortunately, a survey of Soviet literature on the subject yielded little, if any, useful information. According to Soviet authors in the late 1950 and early 1960 coefficients of income elasticity of demand for alcohol ranged from 0.9 to 1.3 [Shvyrkov et al. 1966, p. 229; Beliaevskii et al. eds., 1968, p. 33, pp. 156; Poliakov 1974, p. 64; Rimashevskaia, ed. 1981, p. 35; Maier and Ershov, eds. 1971, p. 93]. However, inconsistencies, ambiguities, and lack of clear definitions of terms and concepts made the use of the data virtually impossible.

12. Professor Mervin Matthews brought to my attention a source which indicated that Soviet statisticians estimated expenditures on "alcoholic beverages, tobacco products, and matches" in the minimal family budget at 5.5 rubles or about 3 percent of the budget (Sarkisian and Kuznetsova 1967, p. 66). In the mid-1960s these three items accounted for about 16 percent of all expenditures on goods in retail trade and kolkhoz urban markets and it therefore appears that the amount allocated is unreasonably small. Accordingly, it was disregarded in the calculations in this study.

13. For the calculations of kolkhoznik expenditures, samogon valued at black market prices was added both on the income and the expenditure sides of the budget.

14. Analysis of alcohol expenditures by republics is made difficult by a puzzling aspect of Soviet retail trade statistics—the sum of republican entries invariably falls short of the USSR total. This unexplained residual accounted for about 1 percent of the total retail trade turnover in the early 1960s and rose to about 2 percent by the late 1970s. One plausible explanation for this residual is that it represents the value of consumer goods distributed centrally, i.e. outside republican trade channels to the Soviet military. Since the sum of alcohol expenditures by republics does not add up to the USSR total, a small downward error is introduced into republican per capita data.

Note on Sources and Bibliographic References Used in the Study

1. Standard Soviet statistical sources published by the Central Statistical Administration (CSA) of the USSR or of union republics such as the annual handbooks of economic statistics *Narodnoe khoziaistvo* are not cited. Thus, whenever a statistic is given in the text without an explanation or a reference it can be found in an appropriate CSA publication.

2. The author used a number of special sources such as communications or interviews with Western visitors to the USSR, Soviet citizens, and recent émigrés from the USSR. In cases when the identity of the source had to be protected, it was done by means of a 9-digit code designed for the general use of the "Second Economy of the USSR" project of the University of California (Berkeley) and Duke University. The supporting documents, communications, notes and tapes are on file with either of the two universities. The use of coded sources in the text is made for the author's reference only and the coded sources are not listed in the bibliography.

3a. Simple, short announcements and newspaper reports are cited in the text by the name of the newspaper and the date of publication but are not included in the bibliography.

3b. References to specific items in the *Bolshaia Sovetskaia Entsiklopedia* ("Large Soviet Encyclopedia") are given in the text by an abbreviated title "BSE," but are not included in the bibliography. The three editions used in this study are as follows: First edition, published between 1926 and 1931, by Aktsionernoe obshchestvo "Sovetskaia entsiklopedia," Moscow; Second edition, published between 1949 and 1958, by Gosudarstvennoe nauchnoe izdatel'stvo BSE, Moscow; Third edition, published between 1970 and 1978, by Izdatel'stvo BSE, Moscow.

3c. References to cartoons published in the Soviet satirical magazine *Krokodil* are given in the text as "Krokodil cartoon" with the number and the year of publication, and the page. These references are not included in the bibliography.

4. A special survey of recent Soviet émigrés by means of a questionnaire is being conducted as a part of the "Second Economy in the USSR" research project at the University of California, Berkeley, and Duke University under the sponsorship of the Ford Foundation. The project is scheduled for completion in early 1983 but the information provided by 533 émigré families whose questionnaires have been processed at the time this monograph went to press has already offered important

insights into various issues related to alcohol in the USSR. The summary results of the questionnaire are described in appropriate sections of the test. The part of the questionnaire covering these issues is appended below.

Appendix: Grossman-Treml Project on Household Budgets in the USSR.

Funded by the Ford Foundation.

Questionnaire

Excerpt of questions pertaining to various issues related to alcohol in the USSR, pp. 25–26, "C" Form. Translated from Russian.

VIII. CONSUMPTION OF ALCOHOL DURING THE LAST NORMAL YEAR[1]

1. How much on the average did your family spend per month on the purchase of alcoholic beverages of state manufacture (at any location: in stores, restaurants, cafes, trains, on vacation, at work, etc.,including purchases made by pooling together, etc.). Recall holidays, birthdays, etc.

   _____ rubles

2. Did you ever buy vodka from middlemen (during prohibited hours or for other reasons)?
   If 'yes,' then:

   Yes ___ No ___

   a. how many liters per month on the average?

   _____ liters

   b. at what average price per half-liter?

   _____ rubles

3. Did you ever purchase moonshine? (Including chacha, etc.)
   If 'yes,' then:

   Yes ___ No ___

   a. how many liters per month on the average?

   _____ liters

   b. at what average price per half-liter?

   _____ rubles

4. Did you or members of your family ever carry out alcohol from your place of work during the last normal year?
   If 'yes,' then how many liters per month on the average?

   Yes ___ No ___

   _____ liters

5. Insofar as you know personally or from reliable sources:

   Never Rarely Often

   a. the production of moonshine in urban localities takes place:

   b. vodka is used as the *primary* means of payment for privately performed work:

   c. vodka is used as supplementary payment for privately per-formed work:

   d. The illegal sale of vodka and other strong liquor in places where such sale is prohibited (stadiums, bathhouses, hospi-tals, etc.), takes place:

   e. the consumption of vodka surrogates (cologne, varnish, industrial alcohol, etc.), takes place:

   f. *Purchasers* of moonshine are fined:

   g. cases when vodka is used as a supplementary payment to insure faster or higher quality work in the state sector take place:

h. In your locality, what served as the raw material for moonshine production? Underline.

a. sugar

b. flour

c. potatoes

d. other vegetables

e. fruit

f. grape mash

g. other materials (specify)

6. Do you personally or otherwise reliably know whether state manufactured vodka contains an admixture of 'non-edible' (or 'synthetic') alcohol?   Yes ___ No ___
   If 'yes,' what kind: (underline)
   a. a product of wood distillation
   b. a product of the distillation of petroleum or gas
   If 'yes',
   c. when did you first learn of it?   in 19___
   d. when did you last learn of it?   in 19___

7. Did you or member of your family use vodka as a payment to stimulate faster or higher quality work in the state sector?   Yes ___ No ___
   If 'yes' how many liters on the average per month in the last normal year?   _____ liters

1. The questionnaire asked the respondents to report all expenditures and income in the "last normal year," i.e. the year before the respondents applied for permission to emigrate from the USSR. As a rule, the status of families who have declared their intention to emigrate changes (loss of jobs, reduced contacts with neighbours, etc.) and hence their experience just prior to departure from the USSR may not be typical.

Bibliography

Alekseev, V. V. and Bukin, S. S. *Rost blagosostoianiia rabochikh Sibiri v usloviiakh stroitel'stva razvitogo sotsializma.* Moscow: Nauka, 1980.

Amalrik, A. *Involuntary Journey to Siberia.* New York: Harcourt Brace Jovanovich, 1970.

Aref'ev, I. I. "Razvitie spirtovoi, likero-vodochnoi i atsetono-butilovoi promyshlennosti na 1959–1965 gg." *Spirtovaia promyshlennost'* 7 (1958): 27–30.

Arens, G. O. "Spirtovaia i likero-vodochnaia promyshlennost' RSFSR v deviatoi piatiletke." *Fermentnaia i spirtovaia promyshlennost'* 2 (1975): 2–5.

Avdonin, L. N., and Burshtein, A. N. "Reshenie zadachi optimal'-nogo razmeshcheniia zavodov po proizvodstvu shampanskogo." *Modeli rezmeshcheniia proizvodstva* Moscow: Nauka, 1975, pp. 55–60.

Babushkin, V. I. "Usilit' kontrol' za raskhodovaniem syr'ia i materialov." *Finansy SSSR* 8 (1974): 24–28.

Bachurin, P. Ia., and Smirnov, V. A. *Tekhnologiia likerno-vodochnogo proizvodstva.* Moscow: Pishchevaia promyshlennost', 1975.

Bakanov, M. I. *Problemy rentabel'nosti torgovli.* Moscow: Ekonomika, 1968.

Balashov, V. E. "O syr'evoi base pivovarennoi promyshlennosti." *Ekonomika sel'skogo khoziaistva* 1 (1976): 106–108.

————— . *Povyshenie effektivnosti pivovarennogo proizvodstva.* Moscow: Pishchevaia promyshlennost', 1979.

Beliaevskii, I. K.; Vasil'ev, V. A.; Mints, L. E.; and Shvyrkov, V. V. eds. *Opyt primeneniia matematicheskikh metodov i EVM v ekonomiko-matematicheskom modelirovanii potrebleniia.* Moscow: Nauka, 1968.

Birman, A. M., ed. *Finansy torgovli* Moscow: Ekonomika, 1970.

Boiko, N. "Uvelichit' proizvodstvo napitkov dlia naseleniia." *Fermentnaia i spirtovaia promyshlennost'* 6 (1979): 2–4.

Boldyrev, E.; Gertsenson, A.; Grishin, B.; Kuznetsova, E.; Mikhailov, A.; Nikiforov, A.; and Iakovlev, A. *Alkogolizm—put' k prestupleniiu.* Moscow: Iuridicheskaia literatura, 1966.

Borisovich, G. F. *Ekonomika promyshlennosti sinteticheskogo kauchuka.* Moscow: Khimiia, 1980.

Bradlee, Benjamin C. *Conversations with Kennedy.* New York: W. W. Norton & Co., 1975.

Burnasheva, I.; Brazhevskaia, T.; and Shul'gina, S. "Bezalkogol'nye napitki i mineral'nye vody." *Kommercheskii vestnik* 12 (1977): 30–32.

Bush, K. "The Soviet Standard of Living." *Radio Liberty Research Paper No. 1.* New York: Radio Liberty Committee, 1964.

————— . "A Comparison of Retail Prices in the United States, the USSR, and Western Europe." *Radio Liberty Research Paper No. 18.* New York: Radio Liberty Committee, 1967.

————— . "A Comparison of Retail Prices in the United States, the USSR, and Western Europe in April 1969." *Radio Liberty Research Paper No. 33.* New York: Radio Liberty Committee, 1969.

————— . "Retail Prices in Moscow and in Four Western Cities in November 1971." *Supplement to Radio Liberty Research Bulletin.* Munich: Radio Liberty, April 19, 1972.

_____ . "Retail Prices in Moscow and Four Western Cities in May 1976." *Osteuropa Wirtschaft* 22 (1977): 122–141.

_____ . "Retail Prices in Moscow and Four Western Cities in March, 1979." *Radio Liberty Research Bulletin Supplement.* Munich: Radio Free Europe—Radio Liberty, July 30, 1979.

Buzulukov, N. S., ed. *Ekonomika i organizatsiia gosudarstvennykh zagotovok produktov sel'skogo khoziaistva.* Moscow: Kolos, 1969.

Bychkov, V. G. *Obshchestvennoe pitanie i aktual'nye voprosy ego razvitiia.* Moscow: Ekonomika, 1978.

Central Intelligence Agency. *Index of Civilian Industrial Production in the USSR. 1950–1961.* (Supplement, CIA/RR 63-29-S) Washington, DC: October 1963.

Chapman, J. G. *Real Wages in Soviet Russia Since 1928.* Cambridge: Harvard University Press, 1963.

Cherliunchakevich, N., ed. *Alkogolizm v sovremennoi derevne.* Moscow: Tsentral'noe statisticheskoe upravlenie, 1929.

Chetyrkin, V. M. "Tainoe vinokurenie v derevne." *Planovoe khoziaistvo* 4–5 (1924): 77–90.

Connor, W. D. "Alcohol and Soviet Society." *Slavic Review* 30 (1971): 570–588.

_____ . *Deviance in Soviet Society: Crime, Delinquency, and Alcoholism.* New York: Columbia University Press, 1972.

_____ . "Alcohol and Soviet Society." In *Beliefs, Behaviors, and Alcoholic Beverages*, edited by M. Marshall. Ann Arbor: University of Michigan Press, 1979, pp. 433–449.

Davies, R. W. *The Development of the Soviet Budgetary System.* Cambridge: Cambridge University Press, 1958.

Davis, C. and Feshbach, M. *Rising Infant Mortality in the USSR in the 1970s.* International Population Reports, series P-95, US Dept. of Commerce, Bureau of the Census, FDAD Washington, D.C.: 1980.

de Lint, J. "The Epidemiology of Alcoholism: The Elusive Nature of the Problem, Estimating the Prevalence of Excessive Alcohol Use and Alcohol-Related Mortality, Current Trends and the Issue of Prevention." In *Alcoholism: A Medical Profile*, edited by N. Kessel, A. Hawker, and H. Chalke. London: B. Edsall and Co. Ltd., 1973.

Denis'ev, V. I., and Ognev, N. N. *Ekonomika, organizatsiia i planirovanie lesokhimicheskikh, gidroliznykh i sul'fitno-spirtovykh proizvodstv.* Moscow: Goslesbumizdat, 1958.

Denshchikov, M. T. "Blizhaishie zadachi nauchno-issledovatel'skikh organizatsii pivo-bezalkogol'noi promyshlennosti." *Spirtovaia promyshlennost'* 6 (1961): 8–11.

Denton, M. E. "Soviet Consumer Policy: Trends and Prospects." In *Soviet Economy in a Time of Change*, Joint Economic Committee, U.S. Congress (Washington, D.C.: Government Printing Office, 1979), pp. 579–789.

"Desiataia piatiletka: god pervyi," *Gidroliznaia i lesokhimicheskaia promyshlennost'* 2 (1976): 1–3.

Dorofeev, V. "Tsena butylki." *Literaturnaia gazeta*, 31 March 1976, p. 13.

_____ . "Chas volka." *Literaturnaia gazeta*, 31 October 1979, p. 8.

Druzhinin, N. K., ed. *Sezonnost' v roznichnoi torgovle i potreblenii.* Moscow: Gosudarstvennoe izdatel'stvo torgovoi literatury, 1963.

Dutton, J. C. "Changes in Soviet Mortality Patterns, 1959–1977." *Population and Development Review* vol. 5, no. 2 (1979): 267–291.

_____ . "Causes of Soviet Adult Mortality Increases." *Soviet Studies* 33 (1981): 548–559.

Efron, V., M. Keller, and Gurioli C. *Statistics on Consumption of Alcohol and on Alcoholism.* New Brunswick: Rutgers Center of Alcohol Studies, 1974.

Elagina, S. S.; Vasilenko, O. V.; and Shesterkina, V. N. *Ekonomika, organizatsiia i planirovanie proizvodstva piva i bezalkogol'nykh napitkov.* Moscow: Pishchevaia promyshlennost', 1975.

F.D.A.D., Bureau of Economic Analysis, U.S. Department of Commerce. *Estimates and Projections of the Population of the USSR by Age and Sex; 1950–2000,* International Population Reports, ser. P-91, no. 23, Washington, DC: U.S. Government Printing Office, 1973.

F.D.A.D., Bureau of the Census, U.S. Department of Commerce. *Population Projections by Age and Sex: 1970 to 2000,* International Population Reports, ser. P-91, no. 26, Washington, DC: U.S. Government Printing Office, 1979.

Fel'dman, I. M. *Roznichnaia torgovlia prodovol'stvennymi tovarami.* Moscow: Ekonomika, 1972.

Feshbach, M. *Demography and Soviet Society.* New York: M. E. Sharpe, Inc., forthcoming 1982.

Field, M. G. and Powell, D. "Alcohol Abuse in the Soviet Union." *The Hastings Center Report.* October 1981, pp. 40–44.

Fridman, A. M. *Ekonomika i planirovanie sovetskoi kooperativnoi torgovli.* Moscow: Ekonomika, 1972.

————. *Ekonomika sovetskoi kooperativnoi torgovli.* Moscow: Ekonomika, 1976.

Gallik, D. M.; Kostinsky, B.; and Treml, V. "Input-Output Structure of the Soviet Economy, 1972." *Foreign Economic Reports,* U.S. Bureau of the Census, Foreign Demographic Analysis Division, Washington, D.C., forthcoming 1982.

Gindikin, V. *Pravda,* 15 January 1979, p. 9 (as cited in *Radio Liberty Research Bulletin,* no. 11, 1 June 1979, p. 1).

Gladkaia, I. I. *Statistika sovetskoi kooperativnoi torgovli.* Moscow: Ekonomika, 1974.

Holzman, F. D. *Soviet Taxation.* Cambridge: Harvard University Press, 1962.

Hyman, M. M.; Zimmerman, M. A.; Gurioli, C.; and Helrich, A. *Drinkers, Drinking and Alcohol-Related Mortality and Hospitalization.* New Brunswick: Center for Alcohol Studies, Rutgers University, 1980.

Keller, M. and Efron V. "Alcohol Problems in Yugoslavia and Russia: Some Observations of Recent Activities and Concerns," *Quarterly Journal of Studies on Alcohol* 35 (1974): 260–71.

Kerashev, M. A. *Mezhotraslevaia kontsentratsiia proizvodstva v pishchevoi promyshlennosti.* Moscow: Pishchevaia promyshlennost', 1971.

Khalaim, A. F. *Tekhnologia spirta.* Moscow: Pishchevaia promyshlennost', 1972.

Khomutov, B. I. *Tovarovedenie prodovol'stvennykh tovarov.* Moscow: Ekonomika, 1970.

Klemenchuk, A. P., and Popov, P. K. *Pishchevaia promyshlennost' RSFSR.* Moscow: Pishchevaia promyshlennost', 1967.

Klianin, V. "Pochem rubli v SSSR." *Novoe russkoe slovo.* 17 November 1980, p. 2.

Kochubeeva, M. T. *Ekonomika, organizatsiia i planirovanie spirtovogo i likerno-vodochnogo proizvodstva.* Moscow: Pishchevaia promyshlennost', 1977.

Kochubeeva, M. T., and Shtainer, A. V. *Ekonomika, organizatsiia i planirovanie proizvodstva no predpriiatiakh likero-vodochnoi promyshlennosti.* Moscow: Pishchevaia promyshlennost', 1974.

Kolobaev, Iu. and Popov, P. *Ekonomika pishchevoi promyshlennosti.* Moscow: Pishchevaia promyshlennost', 1973.

Komarov, V. E, and Cherniavskii, U. G. *Dokhody i potrebelnie naselniia SSSR.* Moscow: Nauka, 1973.

Kondrashev, D. D., and Kondrashov, G. D. *Pribyl', tsena, khozraschet.* Moscow: Mysl', 1969.

Kornienko, V. T. *Tseny i potrebitel'skii spros.* Moscow: Ekonomika, 1964.

Kostin, L. A. *Proizvodstvo tovarov narodnogo potrebleniia.* Moscow: Ekonomika, 1980.

Kovalenko, F. A.; Klots, E. Ia. and Popov, S. I. *O vinogradnykh vinakh i drugikh napitkakh.* Krasnodar: Krasnodarskoe knizhnoe izdatel'stvo, 1974.

Kramarskii, N. A., and Boiko, N. P. "Zadachi spirtovoi, likero-vodochnoi i pivovarennoi promyshlennosti v 1979 g." *Fermentnaia i spirtovaia promyshlennost'.* no. 2 (1979) pp. 2–5.

Krasikov, A. "Tovar nomer odin," *Dvadsatyi vek* (London) no. 2 (1977): 105–150.

Kropotov, V. I. "Rasshiriat' proizvodstvo kormovykh drozhzhei v tselliulozno-bumazhnoi promyshlennosti." *Gidroliznaia i lesokhimicheskaia promyshlennost'.* no. 6 (1968): 1–3.

Kruglikov, A. "Potrebitel'nye svoistva." *Sovetskaia torgovlia.* no. 10 (1971): 39–42.

Kudentsov, N. D. *Tovarovedenie pishchevykh produktov.* 5th ed. Moscow: Ekonomika, 1975.

Kudriavtseva, I. *Tsenoobrazovanie v pishchevoi promyshlennosti.* Moscow: Pishchevaia promyshlennost', 1972.

Kuznetsova, L. "Bolezn' nomer tri." *Literaturnaia gazeta.* 31 March 1976, p. 13.

Lastivkin, V. Ia., ed. *Normativnyi spravochnik po ekonomike i planirovaniiu v sel'skom khoziaistve.* Kishenev: Kartia Moldoveniaske, 1973.

Levin, B., and Levin, M. "Zhenskie charki," *Literaturnaia gazeta.* 20 December 1978, p. 12.

Livshits, S. M., and Iavorskii, V. A. *Sotsial'nye i klinicheskie problemy alkogolizma.* Kiev: Zdorov'e, 1975.

Lokshin, R. *Spros, proizvodstvo, torgovlia.* Moscow: Ekonomika, 1975.

Lulochkin, P. "Trezvost'—norma zhizni." *Nash sovremennik.* 8 (1981): 133–145.

McAuley, A. *Economic Welfare in the Soviet Union.* London: George Allen and Unwin, 1979.

Maier, V. F., and Ershov, E. B. eds. *Differentsirovannyi balans dokhodov i potrebleniia naseleniia i ego ispol'zovanie v planirovanii.* Moscow: Gosplan SSSR, 1971.

Makela, K. *Unrecorded Consumption of Alcohol in Finland, 1950–1975.* Reports from the Social Research Institute of Alcohol Studies, no. 126, Helsinki: The State Alcohol Monopoly, 1979.

Malafeev, A. N. *Istoriia tsenoobrazovaniia v SSSR.* Moscow: Mysl', 1964.

Man'ko, E. "Predlozhili rabochie." *Pravda* 20 October 1980, p. 4.

Matyshevskii, P. S., ed. *Pravovye mery bor'by protiv p'ianstva, alkogolizma i narkomanii.* Kiev: Politizdat, 1980.

Mel'man, M. E.; Misnik, I. A.; Logotkin, I. S.; Sil'ianov, V. G.; Oleinikov, D. G.; Rush, V. A.; Dikker, G. L.; Kliueva, T. K.; and Smotrin, A. A. *Tovarovedenie krakhmala, sakhara, konditerskikh, vkusovykh, molochnykh produktov iz zhirov.* Moscow: Ekonomika, 1966.

Mitin, V. "Interviu s zelenym zmiem," *Krokodil,* no. 18, 1965, p. 13.

Mitiukov, A. D. *Kokteili,* 2nd ed. Minsk: Uradzhai, 1974.

Moreinis, Ia. I *Finansy sakharnoi promyshlennosti.* Moscow: Pishchevaia promyshlennost', 1968.

Nazarian, Sh. G. *Reforma optovykh tsen i problemy dal'neishego sovershenstvovaniia tsenoobrazovaniia v vinodel'cheskoi promyshlennosti SSSR.* Erevan: Gosplan ASSR, 1972.

Neznanskii, F. *Vtoraia ili levaia ekonomika v Sovetskom Soiuze.* New York, 1979. [manuscript, Second Economy project]

Orlovskii, L. "Iad samogona." *Selskaia zhizn',* January 29, 1975, p. 3.

Pal'chuk, V. P. "Formirovanie sebestoimosti produktsii spirtovoi promyshlennosti i dotatsii iz gosudarstvennogo biudzheta." *Khozraschet, finansy i kredit.* no. 20, Kiev-Odessa: Vyshcha shkola, 1978.

Partanen, Iu. "Sotsial'nye problemy sovremennogo burzhuaznogo obshchestva." *Sotsiologicheskie issledovaniia,* no. 1 (1981): 178–186.

Pesni russkikh bardov. vol. 2, Paris: YMCA-Press, 1977.

Poliakov, V. T. "Ob uchete potrebitel'skogo sprosa v roznichnom tsenoobrazovanii." *Vestnik Moskovskogo universiteta.* no. 1 (1974): 57–65.

Popov, P. K. "Ispol'zovanie vtorichnykh material'nykh resursov v pishchevoi promyshlennosti." *Ekonomika pishchevoi promyshlennosti,* 5 (1975): 1–24.

Powell, D. *Alcohol Abuse in the Soviet Union.* Cambridge, Mass.: Harvard University Press, 1983 forthcoming.

Pykhov, V. G. "Spirtovaia, fermentnaia, likero-vodochnaia, pivobezalkogol'naia i atsetonobutilovaia promyshlennost'." *Fermentnaia i spirtovaia promyshlennost',* no. 2 (1964) 4–7.

————. *Ekonomika, organizatsiia i planirovanie spirtovogo proizvodstva.* Moscow: Pishchevaia promyshlennost', 1966.

————. "O realizatsii etilovogo spirta." *Fermentnaia i spirtovaia promyshlennost'.* no. 3 (1969): 27–30.

————. *Ekonomika, organizatsiia i planirovanie spirtovogo proizvodstva,* 2nd ed. Moscow: Pishchevaia promyshlennost', 1973.

Rapawy, S. *Census Data on Nationality Composition and Language Characteristics of the Soviet Population.* U.S. Bureau of the Census, Foreign Demographic Analysis Division, Washington, D.C., May 1980.

"Rasvitie drozhzhevoi promyshlennosti." *Khlebopekarnaia i konditerskaia promyshlennost',* no. 10 (1980: 6–8. (As summarized in *Referativnyi sbornik. Ekonomika promyshlennosti* no. 3, 1981, No. 3G53.)

Riabushkin, T. V., ed. *Uchenye zapiski po statistike. Statisticheskoe izuchenie sprosa i potrebleniia,* vol. 11, Moscow: Nauka, 1966.

Rimashevskaia N. M., ed. *Planovyi differentsirovannyi balanos dokhodov i potrebleniia.* Moscow: Nauka, 1981.

Rimashevskaia, N. M. and Ovsiannikov, A. A., "Potrebitel'skoe povedenie naseleniia: teoriia i rezul'taty modelirovaniia." *Ekonomika i matematicheskie metody,* 17, no. 6: (1981) 85–1094.

Rudavka, S. I., and Michik, V. F., "K voprosu o povyshenii effektivnosti spirtovogo proizvodstva." *Fermentnaia i spirtovaia promyshlennost',* no. 5 (1976): 30–32.

Rutman, A. *Vtoraia ekonomika v SSSR.* New York, 1979. [manuscript, Second Economy project]

Ryzhkov, G. F. *Ekonomika lesokhimicheskoi i gidroliznoi promyshlennosti.* Moscow: Goslesbumizdat, 1961.

Sarkisian, G. S., and Kuznetsova, N. P. *Potrebnosti i dokhod sem'i.* Moscow: Ekonomika, 1967.

Schroeder, G. and Edwards, E., *Consumption in the USSR: An International Comparison.* Joint Economic Committee, U. S. Congress. Washington, D.C.: Government Printing Office, 1981.

Segal, B. *Alkogolizm: klinicheskie, sotsial'no-psikhologicheskie i biologicheskie problemy.* Moscow: Meditsina, 1967.

————. "Drinking Patterns and Alcoholism in Soviet and American Societies: A Multidisciplinary Comparison," in *Psychiatry and Psychology in the USSR*, Edited by S. A. Corson and E. O. Corson. New York: Plenum Press, 1976, pp. 181−266.

Shakhtan, A. S., ed. *Razmeshchenie pishchevoi promyshlennosti SSSR*. Moscow: Pishchevaia promyshlennost', 1969.

Shatunovskii, I. "V polose otchuzhdeniia," *Pravda*, 6 January 1980, p. 6.

Shumskii, D. "Samogonnyi probel." *Pravda*. 16 July 1973.

Shvyrkov, V. V.; Mints, L. E.; and Kuchaev, L. S., eds. *Statisticheskoe izuchenie sprosa i potrebleniia*. Moscow: Statistika, 1966).

Sivolap, I. K.; Molchanova, O. P.; Lobanov, D. I.; Skurikhin, M. A.; Lifshits, M. O.; and Tsyplenkov, N. P., eds. *Kniga o vkusnoi i zdorovoi pishche*. Moscow: Pishchepromizdat, 1954.

Sorokin, G. M.; Oznobin, N. M.; and Zalkind, A. I., eds. *Gruppy A i B promyshlennosti*. Moscow: Ekonomika, 1977.

"Spirtovaia, fermentnaia, likero-vodochnaia, pivo-bezalkogol'naia i atsetono-butilovaia promyshlennost' v 1965 godu." *Fermentnaia i spirtovaia promyshlennost'*, no. 2 (1965): 1−3.

Stabnikov, V. N.; Roiter, I. M.; and Protsiuk, T. B., *Etilovyi spirt*. Moscow: Pishchevaia promyshlennost', 1976.

Stoliarov, S. G. *O tsenakh i tsenoobrazovanii v SSSR*, 2nd ed. Moscow: Gosstatizdat, 1963.

_____ . *O tsenakh i tsenoobrazovanii v SSSR*, 3rd ed. Moscow: Nauka, 1969.

Storchevoi, E. N. "Tekhnicheskoe perevooruzhenie - osnova dal'neishego razvitiia vinodel' cheskoi promyshlennosti," *Vinodelie i vinogradstvo SSSR*, no. 8 (1975): 3−5.

Struev, A. "Sil'nee sukhogo zakona." *Literaturnaia gazeta*, 13 November 1974, p. 12.

Strumilin, S., and Sonin, M., "Alkogol'nye poteri i bor'ba s nimi." *Ekonomika i organizatsiia promyshlennogo proizvodstva*, no. 4: 30−44.

Sulkunen, P. *Developments in the Availability of Alcoholic Beverages in the EEC Countries*. Reports from the Social Research Institute of Alcohol Studies, no. 121, Helsinki: The State Alcohol Monopoly, 1978.

Tartakovskii, E. M. *Planirovanie vinodel'cheskoi promyshlennosti*. Moscow: Pishchevaia promyshlennost', 1966.

Tiraspolsky, A. "Le pouvoir d'achat du rouble en 1972." *Revue de l'Est*, 5, (1974): 79−124.

Tkachevskii, Iu. M. *Pravovye mery bor'by s p'ianstvom*. Moscow: Izdatel'stvo Moskovskogo Universiteta, 1974.

Tovarnyi slovar', Vol. 1−9, Moscow: Gosudarstvennoe izdatel'stvo torgovoi literatury, 1956−1961.

Treml, V. "Alcohol in the USSR: A Fiscal Dilemma." *Soviet Studies*, 35 (1975): 161−77.

_____ . "Production and Consumption of Alcoholic Beverages in the USSR." *Journal of Studies on Alcohol*, 36 (1975): 285−320.

_____ . "Death from Alcohol Poisoning in the USSR." *The Wall Street Journal*, op. ed. page, 10 November 1981.

_____ . "Death from Alcohol Poisoning in the USSR." *Soviet Studies*, 35 (1983): forthcoming.

_____ . Gallik, D. M., Kostinsky, B. L., and Kruger, K. W., *The Structure of the Soviet Economy*. (New York: Praeger Publishers, 1972).

Ts S.U. *Narodnoe khoziaistvo SSSR v 1960 godu. Statistichiskii ezhegodnik*. (Moscow: Gosstatizdat, 1961).

_____ . *Narodnoe khoziaistvo SSSR v 1967 godu. Statistichiskii ezhegodnik*. (Moscow: Statistika, 1968).

Tulebaev, T. *Voprosy teorii i praktiki planirovaniia biudzhetov soiuznykh respublik.* Moscow: Ekonomizdat, 1963.

Turetskii, Sh. Ia. *Ocherkii planovogo tsenoobraznovaniia v SSSR.* Moscow: Gospolitizdat, 1959.

Turgeon, L. *The Contrasting Economies.* Boston: Allyn and Bacon, 1963.

Vaksenberg, A. "Iad pod sudom." *Literaturnaia gazeta.* 15 October 1975, p. 12.

Varibus, V. I.; Zhuk, Iu. T.; Rush, V. A.; and Fedotova, T. K., *Tovarovedenie prodovol'stvennykh tovarov.* Moscow: Ekonomika, 1976.

Vasil'ev S. S., and Fefilov, A. I., eds. *Ekonomika torgovli.* Moscow: Ekonomika, 1968.

Verkhovnyi sud RSFSR. *Sbornik postanovlenii plenuma, presidiuma i opredelenii sudebnoi kollegii po ugolovnym delam.* Moscow: Iuridicheskaia literatura, 1964.

Veselov, I. Ia., and Shakhtan, A. S., *Razvitie pivovarennoi promyshlennosti.* Moscow: Gosizdat, 1955.

Vinogradov, N. V., ed. *Ekonomika pishchevoi promyshlennosti SSSR.* Moscow: Pishchevaia promyshlennost', 1968.

————. *Ekonomika pishchevoi promyshlennosti.* Moscow: Pishchevaia promyshlennost', 1976.

"Vinogradstvo i vinodelie SSSR za 50 let." *Vinodelie i vinogradstvo SSSR.* no. 8 (1972): 2—8.

Vneocherednoi XXI s'ezd KPSS. vol. 2, Moscow: Gospolitizdat, 1959.

Voina, V. "Tsena pokhmel'ia," *Literaturnaia gazeta.* 24 June 1978, p. 12.

Volkov, A. M. "Fond lichnogo potrebleniia v statisticheskom mezhotraslevom balanse." *Ekonomika i matematicheskie metody.* no. 5 (1968): 721—731.

Vol'shanskii, M. I.; Svirida, V. G.; and Iarovenko, V. L., "K istorii proizvodstva vodki v Rossii," *Fermentnaia i spirtovaia promyshlennost',* no. 6 (1977): 39—42.

Voronov, D. N. "Analiz derevenskogo alkogolizma i samogonnogo promysla," *Voprosy narkologii,* no. 1 (1926): 51—70.

Zadorozhnyi, V. K., ed. *Spravochnik torgovogo rabotnika,* 2nd. ed., Kiev: Vyshcha shkola, 1975.

Zaiats, I. N.; Kruzhkova, R. V.; and Petrenko, I. A., *Ekonomika, organizatsiia, i planirovanie vinogel'cheskogo proizvodstva.* Moscow: Pishchevaia promyshlennost', 1969.

————. *Ekonomika, organizatsiia i planirovanie vinodel'cheskogo proizvodstva.* Moscow: Pishchevaia promyshlennost', 1979.

Zhmyrev, L.; and Larionov, G., "Sakharnyi kleshch." *Sotsialisticheskaia industriia,* 6 October 1971, p. 4.

Zotov, V. P. *Pishchevaia promyshlennost' Sovetskogo Soiuza.* Moscow: Pishchepromizat, 1958.

Zotov, V. P.; Antonov, S. F.; Zharskii, A. M.; Zarin, N. A.; Ishkov, A. A.; Kolomiets, F. S.; Naumenko, P. V.; Opatskii, L. V.; Sivolap, I. K.; and Shakhtan, A. S., eds. *Pishchevaia promyshlennost' SSSR.* Moscow: Pishchevaia promyshlennost', 1967.

Index